CHAUCER

THE KNIGHT'S TALE

HARRAP'S ENGLISH CLASSICS

COMUS AND SOME SHORTER POEMS OF MILTON
Edited by E. M. W. TILLYARD, Litt.D., F.B.A., formerly Master of Jesus College, Cambridge, and PHYLLIS B. TILLYARD, M.A., Girton College, Cambridge

MILTON: PARADISE LOST: BOOKS I AND II
Edited by E. M. W. TILLYARD, Litt.D., F.B.A., formerly Master of Jesus College, Cambridge, and PHYLLIS B. TILLYARD, M.A., Girton College, Cambridge

MILTON: PARADISE LOST: BOOKS IX AND X
Edited by E. M. W. TILLYARD, Litt.D., F.B.A., formerly Master of Jesus College, Cambridge

CHAUCER: THE PROLOGUE TO THE CANTERBURY TALES
Edited by R. T. DAVIES, M.A., Lecturer in English Literature, Liverpool University

CHAUCER: THE KNIGHT'S TALE
Edited by J. A. W. BENNETT, M.A., D.Phil., Professor of Mediæval and Renaissance English in the University of Cambridge

CHAUCER: THE PARDONER'S TALE
Edited by NEVILL COGHILL, Merton Professor of English Literature in the University of Oxford, and CHRISTOPHER TOLKIEN, M.A., Fellow of New College, Oxford

CHAUCER: THE NUN'S PRIEST'S TALE
Edited by NEVILL COGHILL, Merton Professor of English Literature in the University of Oxford, and CHRISTOPHER TOLKIEN, M.A., Fellow of New College, Oxford

TWENTIETH-CENTURY NARRATIVE POEMS
Compiled and edited by MAURICE WOLLMAN, M.A.

TEN TWENTIETH-CENTURY POETS
Edited by MAURICE WOLLMAN, M.A.

POEMS OF THE MID-CENTURY
Edited by JOHN HOLLOWAY, M.A., D.Phil., D.Litt., University Lecturer and Fellow of Queens' College, Cambridge

A BOOK OF MODERN PROSE
Edited by DOUGLAS BROWN, M.A., formerly of The Perse School, Cambridge

TWENTIETH-CENTURY SHORT STORIES
Edited by DOUGLAS R. BARNES, Senior English Master, Minchenden School, Southgate, and R. F. EGFORD, Senior English Master, Selhurst Grammar School

NINE TWENTIETH-CENTURY ESSAYISTS
Edited by HAROLD GARDINER, Senior English Master, Bedales School

SELECTED POEMS OF WILLIAM WORDSWORTH
Edited by DONALD DAVIE, Ph.D., Fellow of Gonville and Caius College, Cambridge

TEN CONTEMPORARY POETS
Compiled and edited by MAURICE WOLLMAN, M.A.

A JOUST BETWEEN AN ENGLISH
AND A FRENCH KNIGHT

The incident depicted took place near Calais in 1384. But the
illustration itself (from a manuscript of the Fourth Book of
Froissart's Chronicles) was made in the late fifteenth century, and
the dress and jousting armour are of that date; the illustrator
doubtless exaggerates some of their peculiarities.

British Museum

Chaucer

The Knight's Tale

EDITED BY

J. A. W. BENNETT

*Professor of Mediæval and Renaissance English
in the University of Cambridge*

SECOND EDITION REVISED

GEORGE G. HARRAP & CO. LTD
LONDON TORONTO WELLINGTON SYDNEY

1958

NOTE

The remarks on Chaucer's Life and Work, and the Appendices, are reprinted, with minor alterations, from the edition of the Prologue by R. T. Davies in this series.

First published in Great Britain 1954
by GEORGE G. HARRAP & Co. LTD
182 High Holborn, London, W.C.1

Second Edition, revised, 1958

Reprinted: 1960; 1963; 1964; 1965

Composed in Garamond type and printed by Western Printing Services Ltd., Bristol

Made in Great Britain

CONTENTS

ABBREVIATIONS USED IN THIS EDITION

adj., adjective
adv., adverb
auxil., auxiliary
b., born
c. (circa), about
cf., compare
conj., conjunction
dat., dative
exclam., exclamation
fig., figurative
(O) Fr., (Old) French
gen., genitive
imp., imperative
impers., impersonal
inf., infinitive
It., Italian
l(l)., line(s)
L., Latin
lit., literally
M.E., Middle English
n., noun
O.E., Od English
O.E.D.,Oxford English
   Dictionary

orig., originally
pl., plural
p.p., past participle
pr., present
prep., preposition
pron., pronoun
prp., present participle
pt., preterite
q.v. (quod vide), which see
rel., relative
refl., reflexive
s., *singular*
subj., subjunctive
Tes., Teseida
v., verb infinitive
If no person is given with
   tense and number of a
   verb, the third person is to
   be understood.
In line references to the *Can-*
   terbury Tales the letters
   refer to the groupings of
   the tales in the editions of
   Furnivall and Skeat.

INTRODUCTION

Chaucer's Life and Work

CHAUCER'S relations on his father's side were prosperous wholesale wine-merchants and customs officials. They lived at Ipswich, then a large port on the river Orwell. Geoffrey himself did not become a merchant; when we first hear of him, in 1357, he was in the household of the Countess of Ulster, wife of Lionel, third son of Edward III, the reigning king. He was probably a page; and thus began his career as a courtier, for he is referred to in 1367 as a "yeoman" and later as a "squire," now in the king's own service.

As a squire Chaucer may have had duties as various as making beds or keeping the king's money, bearing messages to foreign courts, or serving at the royal table. He travelled as a diplomat on the Continent, twice, at least, visiting Italy, though there is no evidence that he there or in France met any poets. But the cultures of France and England were then so similar that a poet at the English court, especially since the queen was from Hainault, had no need to travel to become familiar with French poetry. His wife, Philippa, whom he married about 1366 and of whom no more is heard after 1387, was one of the ladies attending Queen Philippa, and she may have come herself with the queen from Hainault.

Like the squire of the Prologue, he went to war against France; he was taken prisoner and ransomed in 1360, being probably then in his late teens. We know nothing certain about his education. It has been suggested on reasonable evidence that the years between 1360 and 1367, about which we know nothing, were spent in part at the Inner Temple studying law and perhaps other subjects too.

Chaucer's income was chiefly derived from patrons; he received annuities from Edward III and Richard II as an officer of their households, and also, for services done, from John of Gaunt, the second son of Edward and uncle to Richard. But he earned further money from various government posts. His average annual income from all sources was about that of an Assistant Secretary in the British Civil Service to-day, but by no means so secure, depending as much on others' favour as on his own efficiency; and though there is no sign that Chaucer was ever destitute, there are suggestions of one or two tight financial corners.

He was Controller of the Customs on Wool and Hides in the port of London from 1374 to 1386, and Controller of the Petty Customs from 1382 to 1386. From 1389 to 1391 he was Clerk of the King's Works at Westminster, the Tower of London, Eltham, Shene, and many other places, organizing building programmes and keeping meticulous inventories of ladles and frying-pans. In his last years he was a 'forester' or official administering a great royal estate at North Petherton in Somerset.

Chaucer was made a J.P. for Kent in 1385, and an M.P. for that county in 1386. He returned to London, however, not long before he died, and was buried in 1400 in Westminster Abbey. He had leased a house near the Abbey after successfully petitioning King Henry IV, who deposed Richard II in 1399, to continue his pension—the last and perhaps most diplomatic piece of business done by a reasonably successful civil servant and courtier.

It may have been Chaucer's wish for more time at his

literary work that led to his leaving the post of Controller of Customs in 1386, soon after which he is generally supposed to have been writing the *Canterbury Tales*. When he became a government official, writing would appear to have been an occupation for his spare time. The *House of Fame*, which describes with unprecedented dexterity and life how Jove's eagle carried a bewildered Chaucer through the heavens, refers to the poet's going home after he has totted up his accounts in the office, there to read himself silly in solitude and at night to compose love poems, though himself not a lover. If the writing of love poetry, elaborately eloquent and concerned with intense and fine feelings, was the spare-time pursuit of a civil servant, as novel-writing was Trollope's, it was an accomplishment desirable in a medieval courtier; and several of Chaucer's formal lover's complaints survive.

He also wrote longer poems concerning love, the *Parliament of Birds*, the *Book of the Duchess*, and the *Legend of Good Women*. These are influenced by the 'dream-allegory,' which was first used in the *Roman de la Rose*, a thirteenth-century French poem which Chaucer himself translated. In such poems the poet falls asleep, often disturbed by love, and the dream which follows and which makes the body of the poem is allegorical. The *Legend of Good Women* extravagantly praises women who were noble in love, and in this it follows the French romantic tradition; but these lives of Cupid's saints are to be given, says the poem, to the English Queen at 'Eltham or at Shene' and were, perhaps, immediately occasioned by the demands of the ladies of the English court. The poem was imposed as a penance, partly for his having written the story of how a lady, Criseyde, was unfaithful to her lover Troilus.

Troilus and Criseyde, Chaucer's most ambitious love poem, and a work perhaps greater than the *Canterbury*

Tales—though the fact that the first is finished, and the second is not, makes it hard to judge fairly—is a tragedy describing how Troilus passed "Fro wo to wele and after out of joye." Based on a version of the story by Boccaccio, it is even more medieval in form and sentiment than its Italian original; yet its subtlety in delineation of character links it with the modern novel, and its concern with human destiny and free will gives it that philosophical seriousness that has always been an element in the greatest English poetry.

It was not Chaucer's vigorous, colloquial, and racy style for which he was famous among his poetical successors, but his rhetorical. Few things could better demonstrate the change in taste between their day and ours. His follower, Hoccleve, for example, compared him with Cicero, the great Roman rhetorician, and lamented that Chaucer's death had deprived England of

> . . . the swetnesse
> Of rethoric: for unto Tullius
> Was never man so like amonges us.

Such praise kept company with reverence for the philosophy of Chaucer's poetry, and one poet called him "superlative . . . in moralitee and eloquence ornate." It is implied that *sentence* (moral teaching) was appropriately accompanied by a 'high' style, which made the teaching delightful.

Elaborate eloquence was felt to be especially attractive in the Middle Ages. Then the cultivated man liked rhetoric. For us rhetoric means very often 'mere words,' and is associated with hollowness and deception. But though this was also sometimes true in the Middle Ages, the art of rhetoric was then, in general, appreciated as the proper instrument for persuading men seriously to the truth, and a noble way to give pleasure.

The art was taught in the universities and by several

systematic text-books. Chaucer refers, though jokingly, to the author of one of them, Geoffrey de Vinsauf (who lived about the end of the twelfth century), in the Nun's Priest's Tale. These text-books took much from the rhetorical treatises of the ancient world, especially from Cicero's *De Inventione* and from a work wrongly attributed to him, *De Rhetorica ad Herrenium*. In Cicero's time such rhetoric was primarily practised by pleaders in the law-courts, but in the Middle Ages its methods were applied to the composition of official, and therefore dignified, letters, and of poetry with a noble subject.

It is natural to use language as persuasively and pleasurably as possible, and to feel certain expressions more appropriate on some occasions than on others. Such 'rhetoric' we all use. When we say, "You could have heard a pin drop," rather than, "There was complete silence," we are using rhetoric. The direct statement is insufficiently powerful and so we evoke our meaning through a startling picture. We do the same in saying, "Dead as a door-nail," but we also add the power of sound in impressing the picture by alliteration.

Text-books, however, systematize and elaborate this natural practice and turn it into an art which we can learn. Thus we study 'figures of speech' and learn, for example, that the persuasive figure used in "Dead as a door-nail" is called a 'simile.' We also find more elaborate rhetorical devices which it is unlikely we should have used spontaneously, such as 'chiasmus'—the neatly reversed word order in the biblical "I cannot dig, to beg I am ashamed," where pattern incises the idea and decorates it.

We find also that some expressions are more appropriate on some occasions than on others. In church, for example, we hear appropriately dignified language that would be unbearably pompous in the living-room. There are also certain proprieties in the conduct of speech-days and legal cases which we accept, and even enjoy, just as scouts and soldiers often practise ceremonial which is not only appropriate but can also be fun.

Thus, when decorum requires it and to give pleasure to those who enjoy dignified formalities, Chaucer will practise a 'figure' of rhetoric called *exclamatio*, a formal 'exclamation' of grief or reproach. In *Troilus and Criseyde* Troilus stands before the palace of Criseyde, now empty because she has left it and him, and cries,

> O paleis desolat,
> O hous of houses whilom best yhight, [called]
> O paleis empty and disconsolat,
> O thow lanterne of whiche queint is the light.

He continues for fourteen lines, varying his descriptions of the house, but using always the same formula. Thus also the beginning of the Prologue is not a simple, direct statement of time and place, but an elaborate series of circumlocutions. Chaucer here is deliberately not calling a spade a spade. He is practising the learned art of rhetoric.

The Canterbury Tales

Chaucer's most popular work, the *Canterbury Tales*, set out to be a dramatic sequence of stories in prose and verse. To enliven a pilgrimage to Canterbury, a group of "sondry folk" agree to tell four stories each on the way, two going and two coming back, the whole entertainment to be organized by the keeper of the inn from which they set out.

But Chaucer appears never to have completed this ambitious project. No pilgrim except the author himself tells more than one story, seven tell none at all (namely, the five Townsmen, the Yeoman, and the Ploughman), and two tales (those of the Cook and Squire) are left unfinished. In the introduction to the tale of the Parish Priest, the Host calls for his tale, saying that "everyman, save thou, hath toold his tale," and adds that only one tale remains to be told to fulfil the Host's "decree." This seems to imply that Chaucer's intention is altered, and that only one tale is expected of each pilgrim; but not even this modified scheme has come down to us complete.

In l. 24 of the Prologue Chaucer says that "fully twenty-nine" pilgrims were at the Tabard. He describes, however, only twenty-seven, and in addition mentions three priests attendant, presumably, on the Lady Prioress. The numbers will not tally, either with or without these three. It may be that "fully" is intended to smooth over the discrepancy, but it is more likely that it shows typical casualness.

It has been suggested that the reference to three priests was not made by Chaucer at all but by an editor—to fill up l. 164, which the author had left unfinished, intending to continue it by describing the character of the Nun Chaplain. No manuscript has any different version of the line, so that the correction, if such it is, must have been made very early. Two points arise from this. First, that it is often difficult to distinguish between corrections made by Chaucer and those made by later hands; in this case there is no proof either way. Secondly, that the variations in the text of the many manuscripts—there are fifty-eight in which the Tales are relatively complete—are only to be explained by the probability that when Chaucer died he left the work in a number of disordered papers, probably not all in one place, some the revisions of others not yet destroyed, and all quite unready for publication as a finished whole. It is likely that some separate tales had circulated among his friends while he was alive, and he may have read some aloud to an audience; but it was not until after his death that friends, eager for more of what they had sampled, and commercial copyists of manuscripts, the publishers of the day, made several attempts at finding Chaucer's intended text and order of tales, and, editing away some of the inconsistencies and omissions, produced versions of the work varying in a few major and many minor respects.

The extant stories are as diverse as the people who tell them. The Knight's Tale is of love and battle, long richly coloured, and noble; the Miller's Tale is fast, vulgar, boisterous with racy detail and comedy; the Prioress's Tale is well-made, short, pious, with appropriate tender sentiments; satire on displays of learning and the misuse of elaborate rhetoric in poetry is built by the Nun's Priest about a sharp, bright fable of the cock who would not take his wife's advice; and the Parish Priest preaches a sermon of solemn warning about the seven mortal sins. Often the tales are obviously appropriate to their tellers, but this could hardly be said of the tales of the Manciple, or Serjeant at Law.

There had been comparable collections of stories[1] before Chaucer, but none is given organic unity by the natural drama of a pilgrimage and its current entertainment. As the pilgrims ride along quarrels appear between some of them, for example, between the Miller and the Reeve, and their tales are told at each other's expense. Perhaps further drama was intended in a discussion from diverse points of view of the relationship of love and marriage, a theme that had always attracted Chaucer. This is suggested by a certain likeness between the subjects of some tales, for example, those of the Wife of Bath, the Merchant, and the

[1] Two, particularly, in Italian: Boccaccio's *Decameron* and Sercambi's *Novelle*. There is no reason to believe that Chaucer knew them.

Franklin. But this can have been, at the most, only part of his intention.

But the general diversity of the tales was, plainly, planned. Introducing the Miller's Tale, Chaucer refers to at least three varieties, stories of common people, pseudo-historical stories about the manners of gentle-folk, and pious and moral tales. He apologizes to his well-bred readers for the first, and tells them to turn the pages till they find the second. At this point he defends the vulgar subject-matter of the Miller's and Reeve's Tales, just as at ll. 725–742 of the Prologue he defends his use of vulgar language on the grounds that he must not be untrue to his art. He must "report" what was told accurately. The man who "reports" ill-breeding is not himself necessarily ill-bred.[1]

Though it is clear that the author enjoys his characters and situations, high and low, moral and immoral, we are bidden not to make "earnest of game." We are bidden not to judge of the morals and proprieties by which Chaucer regulated his everyday life from this practice of what Keats called "negative capability." And, indeed, in the retraction following the Parson's Tale, which has every appearance of being written to make an earlier end to the sequence than was at first intended, Chaucer deliberately revokes all those tales that "sownen into synne." For his soul's health he finally renounced works in which he had shown his chief strength as an artist.[2] In final "earnest" he renounced the "game." [R.T.D.]

---

[1] The same excuse is made in *Roman de la Rose*, ll. 15159 ff., and by Boccaccio in the *Conclusione* of the *Decameron*.

[2] Many other medieval authors feared eventually that they had offended God, and quieted their consciences in the same way by retracting what they had written.

The Knight's Tale

THOUGH Chaucer nowhere acknowledges his source, it is certain that he derived the tale he puts into the mouth of the Knight from the *Teseida Delle Nozze D'Emilia*, a romantic epic in twelve books of eight-line stanzas, written in 1340 by his Italian contemporary Giovanni Boccaccio (1313?–75).[1] It was to Boccaccio, also, that Chaucer owed the substance of his great poem *Troilus and Criseyde*, which is related to the Italian poet's *Il Filostrato* in much the same way as the Knight's Tale is to the *Teseida*. Boccaccio had written both these poems while paying court to a lady of Naples, where he lived from 1340 to 1350; and both were meant especially for her ears and eyes. Chaucer had no such private purpose, and his versions differ accordingly. But they also show more complex and more interesting differences. While preserving the main outlines of Boccaccio's stories, and most of his fine effects—for Boccaccio has his own poetic virtues, to which the English poet was fully alive—Chaucer has turned them to his own purposes; has altered details to suit his own sense of narrative; and has imbued the whole with his own courtly grace, humour, philosophy, and feeling for the variety of human character.

The Knight's Tale is far from being a translation of the *Teseida*; it is told in 2250 lines as against Boccaccio's 9896; even so, it is the longest of the Canterbury Tales, save for the Parson's prose sermon at the close. Many of Chaucer's lines follow the Italian faithfully and many more show a general correspondence. On the other hand, several pass-

---

[1] Chaucer nowhere mentions the Italian poet by name, and the MSS. he used may have been anonymous; but it is unlikely that he never discovered the identity of their author. That Chaucer (and Boccaccio) had read the French *Roman de Thèbes* is probable but not proveable.

ages¹ and countless details are entirely new. Some stanzas
of the *Teseida* not represented in the Tale Chaucer has em-
bodied in other poems. Adaptations of some sixteen are
found in his *Parlement of Foules* (see note, l. 1060) and of an-
other five in the closing lines of *Troilus and Criseyde* (see
note, l. 1951). Another compressed version of the opening
stanzas of Book Two of the *Teseida* (the source of ll. 1–16)
is found in Chaucer's unfinished *Anelida and Arcite*. As it
stands, this poem tells the story of Arcite's faithlessness
to Queen Anelida, and 240 of 357 lines are given to the
Queen's lamentations.² Her lover has little in common
with the Arcite of the Knight's Tale except the name.
Chaucer perhaps once intended to incorporate in this poem
other passages of the *Teseida*, such as the description of the
temple of Mars (see note, l. 1112); the poem stops just at
the point where Anelida

> unto Mars avoweth sacrifice
> Withinne the temple, with a sorrowful chere,
> That shapen was as ye shal after here. (355–357.)

His decision to make a complete version of the *Teseida* may
have been one of the reasons why *Anelida and Arcite* was
never finished. In the Prologue to the *Legend of Good
Women* Alceste pleads to Cupid on Chaucer's behalf that

> He made the book that hight the Hous of Fame,
> And eke the Deeth of Blaunche the Duchesse,
> And the Parlement of Foules, as I gesse,
> And al the love of Palamon and Arcite
> Of Thebes, though the storye is knowen lite. (F416–421.)

These last two lines must refer to some complete version of
the *Teseida*. Such a version must have been in existence

---

¹ *E.g.*, ll. 176 ff., 304 ff., 393 ff., 511 ff., 1951 ff., 2129 ff.
² L. 1863 of the Tale is identical with l. 287 of *Anelida and Arcite*,
and ll. 1359 ff. closely resemble ll. 325–327.

before this Prologue was written and presumably before the plan of the Canterbury Tales was conceived. Critics have supposed that the phrase "of that storie list me not to write" (343) is evidence that the Tale was rather casually adapted from an earlier version not intended for a narrator. It is indeed likely that Chaucer made some alterations when he decided to place the story of Palamon and Arcite in the mouth of a Knight, and we can make reasonable guesses as to what they were; but we have no means of checking our guesses since no earlier version survives.

This 'medievalization' of a story set in classical Greece is by no means confined to the feats and arms of chivalry; it is to be noted in Chaucer's description of such incidents as Theseus's triumphal return to Athens on horseback (like any medieval king) instead of in the classical chariot mentioned by Statius and Boccaccio; or the observance that Emily and Arcite do to May. And much that is medieval (or, as it would seem to Chaucer's contemporaries, modern) in the tale's tone and temper, was present already in Boccaccio's version of the story. Neither poet is much troubled by a sense of anachronism. Chaucer gives in a line a simple justification for describing the knights of ancient Greece as, like his own knight, decked "in a habergeoun and in a light gipoun," or carrying prussian shields:

> There is no newe gise that it nas old.

It is not that the medieval mind completely lacked 'historical sense' or any awareness that, as Chaucer himself puts it in *Troilus and Criseyde*:

> . . . for to winnen love in sondry ages,
> In sondry londes, sondry ben usages;

but that differences in costume and custom were felt to be trifling compared with the emotions and activities that the ancient and medieval world had in common. There was little or no sense of a barrier between the pagan past and the Christian present, and long before the fourteenth century the study of classical poetry and story had, by various means, been made completely 'respectable'; and writers of the Middle Ages found, or thought they found, resemblances in the classical world to their own ideals and their own society. Even the pagan deities had been given allegorical or, as we see in the *Knight's Tale*, astrological roles: the planets named after them being credited with qualities resembling theirs. Chaucer can thus admit them as powerful if anthropomorphic deities, while at the same time using the characters and structure of the tale itself to express his own view of Divine wisdom and purpose, without employing any specifically Christian phraseology. He equates Jupiter with the Prime Mover, and gives to Theseus in his final speech sentiments that, while acceptable to Chaucer's contemporaries, derived their essence from Greek philosophy. Here there is nothing to jar on 'historical sense'—modern or medieval. He knew well enough that Theseus, Palamon, and Arcite belonged to the distant and legendary past; and he wished to give the effect of distance, in place and time. Thus, to obtain particular effects of strangeness and wonder he takes over from Boccaccio details that had no counterpart in medieval life— such as Lycurgus's chariot of gold drawn by four white bulls (1281). He even adds such details of his own accord —for example, the tame lions and leopards that run about the great Emetreus, King of Ind (1328). In short, he knew exactly when and how far to modernize or expand, and when to leave unaltered Boccaccio's blend of pagan and contemporary.

At the very beginning of his tale the Knight refers to "olde stories" as authority for Theseus's exploits; and early scribes indicated the stories that Chaucer had in mind when they added in the margin a quotation from Statius's *Thebaid*. The reputation of Statius in the Middle Ages was great; and Chaucer elsewhere ranks him with Virgil, Homer, Ovid, and Lucan (*Troilus and Criseyde V*, 1792). At the beginning of the *Teseida* Boccaccio acknowledges indebtedness to the *Thebaid*; and this if nothing else would prompt Chaucer to glance at it while preparing his version of Boccaccio's poem. But the *Thebaid*, though it mentions Theseus, has nothing to say of Palamon or Arcite; and Chaucer's indebtedness to it in this tale is probably limited to a few of the opening lines (*e.g.*, 112, 122) and to phrases in the description of the Temple of Mars (see note, l. 1112).

More certain, more pervasive, and more important is the influence of Boethius's book *De Consolatione Philosophiae*. Boethius, a Christian philosopher (though this book contains no specifically Christian doctrine), wrote in the sixth century A.D. Throughout the Middle Ages the prestige and influence of his work were immense, and Chaucer's study and translation of it seem to have been responsible for the views on the destiny of man to which the characters in this poem—and others of his—give utterance. Most of the philosophical seriousness manifested in the speeches and soliloquies of the main characters is due ultimately to Boethius (see notes to ll. 393, 2129); and by giving this philosophical tinge to the story as he found it in Boccaccio, Chaucer unobtrusively alters its total effect. Boethius, too, could provide hints as to how to consider the ways of Providence without using specifically Christian expressions such as would have seemed incongruous in the mouth of a Theseus or a Palamon.

The Knight comes first in the series of pilgrims described in the Prologue, not only because he was the highest in the

social scale, but also because he embodied the virtues that
signify a noble life:

> Trouthe and honour, fredom and curteisye . . .

The rest of the pilgrims would think it as fitting as Chaucer
did that "whether by adventure, or sort, or cas," the cut
fell to this modest hero. And they would have other
reasons besides a sense of decorum for being "ful blithe
and glad" that he "began the game." As a knight, he was
likely to have travelled far; and his gipoun, "al bismotered
with his habergeoun," was evidence enough that he had
just come from the wars. Who more likely or better qual-
fied to tell a story new to them all, of romance and adven-
ture, such as he might well have learnt—as Chaucer him-
self had done—beyond the perilous seas? In the persons
of the knight and his son the motley band would see
romance personified; and no audience could be more apt
for such a tale than a company of pilgrims breathing the
bright air of spring and engaged on what was for some of
them the greatest adventure of their lives, and for all a
notable journey. And whether or not we suppose that the
Knight would have won the supper "at oure aller cost,"
we can be sure that his tale represents that blend of "best
sentence and moost solaas" which the Host looked for—a
requirement that some of the later story-tellers tend to
forget. We are not surprised to learn that when the tale
was done

> In al the route nas ther yong ne oold
> That he ne seide it was a noble storye
> And worthy for to drawen to memorye;
> And namely the gentils everichoon—

"especially the gentlefolks," who would delight in a
romantic story that gave due place to the virtues of a
"gentil herte."

We must not press Chaucer's 'dramatic intention' too far: and this is not the place to consider by what means he creates the illusion that these are 'real' travellers listening to 'real' stories and story tellers. But whatever our judgment on the dramatic fitness of the later tales, there can be little doubt that he turned to frame the Knight's Tale with the happy consciousness that this "olde storye" from the "Grete See," where the Knight himself had fought, could be exactly suited to the noblest of the pilgrims and equally suited to the Host's injunction that the tales should be "of aventures that whilom han befalle." Its very first line reminds us of this, just as the succeeding lines describing Theseus,

> What with his wisdom and his chivalrye,
> He conquered al the regne of Femenye
> That whilom was ycleped Scithia,

recall the initial picture of the courteous Knight in the Prologue who "loved chivalrye" and was not only "worthy" but "wis." Already we are over the Kentish hills and far away, in place and time. Henceforward an occasional explanatory phrase, a technical detail, are enough to keep the character of the narrator before us, and to preserve the knightly tone. We have hardly gone thirty lines before we are reminded of his modesty—"waike been the oxen in my plough"—and then of his courtesy to all sorts and conditions of men—"I wol nat letten eek noon of this route." He who "nevere yet no vileinye ne saide" speaks with horror of Creon's "vileinye" (84). The "parfit gentil knight" describes his own hero Theseus as "a trewe knight" who will defend the cause of the widows; and he cannot forbear to add that as Theseus sets out "by his baner born is his *penoun*" (which, like any medieval warrior's, displays his cognizance). It is the same narrator who —again without any hint from Boccaccio—shows Theseus

as shocked by a duel "withouten juge or oother officere"
(854), but content when he can arrange a proper combat in
good set terms like "Armed for listes up at alle rightes"
(994); swearing "upon my trouthe, and as I am a knight"
to be "evene juge, and trewe" (1006). It is the young
Squire's father who speaks delightedly of the lusty knights
who "wolde, hir thankes, wilnen to be there" (1253 ff.);
who dilates in technical terms on the preparations for the
tourney:

> Nailinge the speres, and helmes bokelinge,
> Gigginge of sheeldes, with layneres lacinge; (1645–46)

on the combat itself:

> Ther seen men who can juste and who can ride.
> Ther shiveren shaftes upon sheeldes thikke; (1746 ff.)

on grim details he had himself observed on many a field;
and on the tragic outcome:

> As blak he lay as any cole or crow,
> So was the blod yronnen in his face . . .
> Tho was he corven out of his harneis,
> And in a bed ybrought ful faire and blive. (1834–39.)[1]

To refer to Theseus as the hero of the Knight's story
may seem inexact; and one critic has described him in
much less complimentary terms: "sometimes cruel, if not
actually brutal, . . . hints of selfish motives." But his
blend of humorous wisdom and sane realism certainly
makes him the most 'Chaucerian' of the characters. In his
speeches there is a dignity (even, in the last speech, a
profundity) that we do not sense in those of Boccaccio's
Teseo; yet at the same time they are lively, terse, delightful,
suffused with Chaucer's own humour and sanity:

[1] Cf. also 1342, 1772.

> She, for whom they han this jolitee,
> Can hem therefore as muche thank as me;
> She woot namoore of al this hoote fare,
> By God, than woot a cokkow or an hare.

And again,

> Ye woot yourself she may nat wedden two
> At ones, though ye fighten everemo.
> That oon of you, al be him looth or lief,
> He moot pipen in an ivy leef!

This same blend of dignity and common sense also appears when we see Theseus in action. Impetuous and impulsive, quickly touched—in Chaucer's version of the story—to pity or to anger, he suddenly sets out to revenge wronged widows just as he is about to enter Athens after a long absence. He breaks in on the duelling rivals with a

> . . .'Hoo!
> Namoore, upon peine of lesinge of youre heed';

condemns them out of their own mouths, and then, because he is a reasonable man who can remember his own follies, forgives them. His matter-of-fact humour appears as all of a piece with his ability to 'make a virtue of necessity.' Yet Chaucer, at the same time that he makes Theseus more human than his Italian original, makes him more god-like. For in his wisdom and equity (Chaucer makes him say, "I wol be trewe juge, and no partye") and in his function as an arbiter of Fate he comes much nearer than Teseo to the divine ruler, to the Jupiter who arbitrates among the Gods, the First Mover whose "greet effect" and "heigh entente" he himself extols.[1] Chaucer seems consciously to shape Boccaccio's duke into something closer to what the Knight's own concept of an ideal prince would be: one fond of 'chivalry' in the medieval sense of

---

[1] Cf. l. 1671—Chaucer's addition.

martial prowess and array, fonder still of justice, capable of pity, and inclined to mercy; fulfilling, in short, the knightly code as it was to be set forth by Sir Thomas Malory: "Always to flee treason, and to give mercy unto him that asketh mercy . . . and always to do ladies, damsels, and gentlewomen and widows succour, and strengthen them in their rights."

Chaucer's characterization of Palamon and Arcite likewise shows some reshaping of material provided by Boccaccio. The rivals are not sharply distinguished in the *Teseida*, except in a somewhat conventional description in stanzas 49–50 of the third book, where Palemone is described as "strong-limbed, clever in speech, subtle, solemn in movement, and bold" and Arcita as "rather slender, fair, open in speech, and dextrous." Chaucer omits these details, and in some other ways seems to approximate the rivals to each other rather than to differentiate between them. He does, it is true, retain the contrast between the ardent Palamon who cares not whether he win victory, "so that I have my lady in mine armes," and the martial Arcite who prays only for victory. He deliberately alters Boccaccio's account of their first glimpse of Emily: giving the first view of her to Palamon, who is the only one of the pair, in Chaucer, to describe her as "Venus" (l. 244; in Boccaccio Arcite too says that it is she); and something of the medieval lover's devotion to Love as a religion characterizes Palamon's subsequent words and deeds: whereas a certain naked self-interest appears in the Arcite who can say:

> And therfore at the kinges court, my brother,
> Ech man for himself, ther is noon oother. (323–324.)

But Chaucer is more interested in their situation than in their personalities. One of the elements in that situation is the conflict between the claims of love and the claims of sworn brotherhood; and though Arcite puts love above 'brotherhood,' he does not abjure the chivalry out of which the sense of brotherhood sprang. Chaucer alters the details of the story so that Arcite's magnanimity can appear in his promise to bring armour for them both:

> And chees the beste, and leve the worste for me. (756.)

And before the fight in the woods Chaucer reminds us again of their friendship:

> Everich of hem heelp for to armen oother,
> As freendly as he were his owene brother (793–794.)

For the rest, each is made more eminently a lover living by the code of lifelong fidelity to a mistress. Each might have used the words that Chaucer puts into the mouth of another of love's servants:

> Whos I am al, and evere wol hir serve,
> To what hir lest, to do me live or sterve;
>
> Besekinge hir of merci and of grace,
> As she that is my lady sovereine.
> *(Parlement of Foules,* 419–421.)

Arcite is described as a prey to the lovers' malady of *hereos* (see note, 503–520), Palamon as likewise 'mad' with love. Whereas in Boccaccio the entire action takes place within a few years, in Chaucer seven years pass before the lovers come close to the consummation of their hopes. Each is carefully balanced against the other. Each in turn ponders the decrees of Destiny (*e.g.,* ll. 228 ff., 445 ff.). Each in the end can think kindly of the other.

The differences between Boccaccio's Emilia and Chaucer's Emilye are more obvious. Emilia is artful and coy. When she realizes that the two prisoners are looking at her from their window she acts according to the typically Boccaccian sentiment that "la vanitate innata han le femine

nel core" ('vanity is innate in woman's heart'). She sees
Arcita leave the prison, and thinks what a personable
young man he is; later, she guesses his identity beneath his
disguise; and it is she, not Teseo, who comes upon him
and Palemone fighting in the forest. Chaucer omits all such
incidents, so that his heroine differs from Boccaccio's some-
what as his Criseyde differs from Boccaccio's attractive
Italian young lady of the same name. But whereas in
Troilus and Criseyde Chaucer has lavished all his art on
Criseyde while presenting Troilus as all that a courtly lover
ought to be, in the Knight's Tale he pays most attention
to the emotions of the male lovers, and sets their mistress
in the background. She has the charm of a figure from an
illuminated manuscript of a French romance; but she is
also the English prototype of the passive heroine; the
Edith of Scott's *Old Mortality* is her lineal descendant; and
Scott, it is worth noting, remembered Chaucer's tale when
writing that story of rival lovers—just as he remembered
it when he came to describe the tournaments in *Ivanhoe*.

Teseida

*A summary indicating the main differences in Boccaccio's version of
the story.*

Book I begins with an invocation to the Muses and to Mars,
Venus, and Fiammetta (Boccaccio's mistress). In 138 stanzas
it tells of Teseo's war with the Amazons and his marriage to
Ipolita; noticing the beauty of Ipolita's little sister Emilia, he
plans to marry her to his kinsman Acate.

Book II. After two years' absence Teseo, having been re-
proached by Peritoo (Pirithous), in a vision, for dallying, returns
to Athens with Ipolita and Emilia. Entering the city in his
chariot he finds the throng of widows in the temple of Clemency.

Evannes (Evadne) tells how Creon denies burial to their husbands' bodies, which are eaten by animals. Teseo addresses his knights and they follow the widows to Thebes. After killing and burying Creon, he gives license to pillage. The widows depart with their husbands' ashes; and the Greeks find the wounded Arcita and Palemone, who explain that they are of Cadmus's blood. Teseo has his doctors tend them, and when he returns to Athens in triumph they go before his chariot. Later he condemns them to a life imprisonment, but in comfortable quarters within his palace.

Book III begins with an invocation to Cupid. In the spring Emilia, while singing love-songs in the garden, is heard by Arcita, who, without saying anything to Palemone, goes to the window and forthwith cries out: "Palemone, come and see! Venus has come down to us." Palemone agrees, and both say that Cupid has wounded them. Emilia, aware that she is noticed, withdraws, but thereafter watches their window, breaking into song whenever she thinks they may be watching. At first they wonder whether she is goddess or woman, but soon learn her identity from their servant. They grow desperate with love, but do not quarrel.

Peritoo, during a visit to Teseo, recognizes his old friend Arcita, and procures his release on condition that he never sets foot in the kingdom again. Arcita thanks Teseo in ambiguous terms, saying that "love has bound me to you and yours." Teseo gives him gifts on his departure. He takes a sad farewell of Palemone. As he rides away Emilia appears on a balcony and is touched by his appearance.

Book IV. Arcita goes to Bœotia, with a retinue, and changes his name to Penteo. He journeys to Thebes, where he laments the fate of his family, and finally reaches Aegina (an island near Athens), where he hopes to learn news of Emilia. Hearing that Acate, to whom she had been betrothed, is dead, and being greatly altered in appearance by his love-sickness, he takes ship for Athens, where he prays in the Temple of Apollo that he may not be recognized, and receives a sign that his prayer is granted. He takes service with Teseo, and recovers health and strength. Emilia alone recognizes him, but pretends that she had not seen him before, and that she does not know that he is in love with her. He makes his secret laments to Fortune and his prayers to Phoebus and Venus in a grove three miles from Athens. There one morning Panfilo, a servant of Palemone, overhears him soliloquizing about his disguise, and informs his master.

Book V. Jealousy had begun to stir in Palemone at the thought that perhaps Emilia had procured Arcita's release. At first he does not credit Panfilo's story, but later determines to get out of prison and win Emilia by arms. He feigns sickness. Panfilo brings a Theban physician into prison to attend to him, intoxicates the guards, and changes clothes with Palemone who leaves the prison with the physician, goes to an inn, procures a horse and arms, and finds Arcita asleep in the grove. Arcita soon recognizes him, and they talk in friendly fashion until they begin to dispute about Emilia, when Palemone insists on settling the quarrel by the sword. Arcita reluctantly arms himself, and mounts his horse. In the ensuing fight Arcita deals Palemone a blow that seems likely to be mortal; but while Arcita grieves over him and complains, "Why did I ever love?" Palemone recovers, and they charge each other again "like dragons." Teseo and Emilia enter the grove with a company ahawking and ahunting, and by chance Emilia comes upon the combatants. Recognizing her, they fight more fiercely than ever, until she summons Teseo. After watching them for a while he inquires who they are, and Arcita agrees to tell him on condition of his promising them his 'peace'; which he grants. They tell him their names, and the cause of their dispute, and Teseo, out of pity, pardons them. He thinks that both are worthy of Emilia, but, as she cannot have both, imposes the condition of a tournament "in our theatre" a year hence. To this they agree, and return to Athens with him.

Book VI. They spend the year there amicably, holding jousts,

trying to win Emilia's favour, and summoning friends for the
tourney—among them Lycurgus, Peleus, Nisus, Agamemnon,
Menelaus, Castor and Pollux, and many others whose names and
appearance are given.

Book VII. When the day draws near Teseo addresses all the
company in the theatre, saying that he had not intended such a
concourse, but only a 'palæstral game'; he wished the tourney
to be friendly and not bitter; and therefore only swords and
maces are to be used.

The day before the tourney Arcita visits the temples of the
gods, and prays to Mars for victory. His prayer ascends to the
historiated house of Mars in the cold fields of Thrace. Palemone
likewise visits the temples, making special prayers to Cytherea.
His prayer goes to her temple on Mount Cithæron, set in a pleas-
ant garden, and sees Venus naked in the temple. The resultant
strife between Venus and Mars is settled by 'masterly cunning.'
When Emilia prays to Diana she is told that it has been decided
among the gods whom she shall wed. She passes an anxious
night, but rises more beautiful than the morning star.

In the morning Teseo takes Palemone and Arcita to do sacri-
fice in the temple of Mars. Before the tournament he announces
that those captured in the fight shall lay down their arms, and
that the one who is victorious shall have the lady.

Book VIII. Many of the single combats are described in great
detail, and the names of the combatants given. Ipolita, as she
watches, yearns to join the fight; but Emilia thinks that the
souls of the dead knights will haunt her: "Each of the rivals is so
handsome that I don't know which I would choose. Oh that
Teseo had let them fight on when we found them in the grove!"
Mars and Venus watch from above, and Mars, speaking through
Teseo, taunts Arcita with cowardice. Palemone is bitten by a
horse, so that he falls, and Arcita disarms him. Emilia's heart
now turns towards Arcita.

Book IX. Venus now says to Mars, "Thy part is finished," and

sends Erinis in front of Arcita's horse, so that he falls. Emilia
grows pale at this, and Palemone grieves for him—and for him-
self. Arcita is taken to the palace in a triumphal car, with Emilia,
who comforts him. Teseo announces that all of Palemone's men
can go free, and that Palemone is Emilia's prisoner. She gives
him his liberty, and a ring. Arcita asks for Emilia, and the pair
are betrothed.

Book X. The corpses are burnt. Arcita begs Teseo that Emilia
shall be given to Palemone if he dies, but Emilia says that she
will never wed another. After nine days of suffering Arcita
sacrifices to Mercury, praying him to take his soul gently away.

Book XI. Arcita's soul goes to the concavity of the eighth
heaven, whence he looks down at the little earth and laughs at
the mourning made for him. Emilia cries " Where art thou?
I would follow thee." No one can console Teseo or his father
Egeo (Egeus).

Palemone cuts his beard and hair and casts them on to Arcita's
pyre, with arms and jewels. Egeo places the ashes in the temple
of Mars, pending the building by Palemone of a temple to Juno
on the site of the pyre; in this temple are portrayed all the adven-
tures of Palemone and Arcita.

Book XII. Emilia grows pale and thin. After several days it is
agreed that she shall marry Palemone. Teseo urges this course
on Palemone, but he demurs, saying that his love for Arcita will
not allow him to render 'villainy' for Arcita's 'courtesy.' At
length he prays to Jove, Diana, Cytherea, and to the soul of
Arcita, begging him to pardon him for obeying Teseo. Emilia,
too, at first demurs, saying that she is dedicated to Diana, who
has already taken vengeance on Acate and Arcita. Teseo replies
that if Diana had been angry she would have visited her anger on
Emilia.

All change their mourning garments and go to the temple of
Venus (Emilia decked in green). The feasting lasts fifteen days,
and then the visitors depart.

A farewell address to the book:

> You, O my book, are the first to make the muses sing the lofty
> struggles of Mars in the common tongue. Since you are the
> first to plough these waves perhaps you will stand worthy of
> some honour. Here we lower our wandering sails, and await
> at anchor the garlands and gifts that are our due.

A Note on the Text

The text is based on the manuscript formerly belonging to
Lord Ellesmere, and now in the Henry E. Huntington Library,
San Marino, California. Departures from this MS. (which is
referred to as *El*) are recorded in the footnotes, along with a
selection of variant readings from other manuscripts, in
particular:

Hg = Hengwrt MS. 154, now in the National Library of
Wales, Aberystwyth.

Gg = Cambridge University Library MS. Gg.4.27.

Cp = Corpus Christi College, Oxford MS. 188.

El and *Hg* were probably written in the first decade of the
fifteenth century, *Cp* in the second, and *Gg* in the third or
fourth.

All readings are taken from the Chaucer Society's print of
these MSS., corrected in respect of the Ellesmere text from the
facsimile edition of that manuscript and from collations pub-
lished by E. Flugel and D. Everett. Omissions that are probably
accidental are not usually noted.

The following changes have been made in the spelling found
in the MSS.:

i, ai, ei, oi are regularly printed instead of *y, ay, ey, oy* (and *vice
versa*) when this procedure helps the modern reader to identify
the form: *e.g., knight, reine* for MS. *knyght, reyne*.

As regards *c* and *k*, *i* and *j*, *u* and *v*, the text conforms as far as
possible to modern usage.

Final *-tz* is printed as *ts* (e.g., *servants* for *seruantz*).

The variant forms of the final *-r(e)* in *hir(e)* are all represented
by *-r*.

THE KNIGHT'S TALE

WHILOM, as olde stories tellen us,
Ther was a duk that highte Theseus;
Of Atthenes he was lord and governour,
And in his time swich a conquerour,
That gretter was ther noon under the sonne.
Ful many a riche contree hadde he wonne;
What with his wisdom and his chivalrye,
He conquered al the regne of Femenye,
That whilom was ycleped Scithia,
And weddede the queene Ypolita,   10
And broghte hir hoom with him in his contree
With muchel glorye and greet solempnitee,
And eek hir faire¹ suster Emelye.
And thus with victorye and with melodye
Lete I this noble duk to Atthenes ride,
And al his hoost, in armes him biside.

   And certes, if it nere to long to heere,
I wolde you have toold fully the manere
How wonnen was the regne of Femenye
By Theseus, and by his chivalrye;   20
And of the grete bataille for the nones
Bitwixen Atthenes and Amazones;
And how asseged was Ypolita,
The faire, hardy queene of Scithia;
And of the feste that was at hir weddinge,
And of the tempest at hir hoom-cominge;

¹ *Other MSS.* yonge.

But al that thing I moot as now forbere.
I have, God woot, a large feeld to ere,
And waike been the oxen in my plough.
The remenant of the tale is long ynough.   30
I wol nat letten eek noon of this route;
Lat every felawe telle his tale aboute,
And lat se now who shal the soper winne.
And ther I lefte, I wol ayein biginne.

    This duk, of whom I make mencioun,
Whan he was come almoost unto the toun,
In al his wele and in his mooste pride,
He was war, as he caste his eye aside,
Wher that ther kneled in the weye[1]
A compaignye of ladies, tweye and tweye,   40
Ech after oother, clad in clothes blake;
But swich a cry and swich a wo they make,
That in this world nis creature livinge
That herde swich another waymentinge;
And of this cry they nolde nevere stenten,
Til they the reines of his bridel henten.

    'What folk been ye, that at min hom-cominge
Perturben so my feste with cryinge?'
Quod Theseus. 'Have ye so greet envye
Of min honour, that thus compleine and crye?   50
Or who hath yow misboden, or offended?
And telleth me if it may been amended;
And why that ye been clothed thus in blak.'

    The eldeste lady of hem alle spak,
When she hadde swowned with a deedly cheere,
That it was routhe for to seen and heere,

        [1] *Other MSS.*, h(e)igh(e) weye.

She[1] seide: 'Lord, to whom Fortune hath yeven
Victorye, and as a conquerour to liven,
Nat greveth us youre glorye and youre honour;
But we biseken mercy and socour.   60
Have mercy on oure wo and oure distresse.
Som drope of pitee, thurgh thy gentillesse,
Upon us wrecched wommen lat thou falle.
For certes, lord, ther is noon of us alle,
That she ne hath been a duchesse or a queene;
Now be we caitives, as it is wel seene:
Thanked be Fortune, and hir false wheel,
That noon estaat assureth to be weel.
And certes, lord, to abiden youre presence,
Heere in the temple of the goddesse Clemence   70
We han ben waitinge al this fourtenight;
Now help us, lord, sith it is in thy might.
I, wrecche, which that wepe and waille[2] thus,
Was whilom wif to King Cappaneus,
That starf at Thebes, cursed be that day!
And alle we, that been in this array,
And maken al this lamentacioun,
We losten alle our housbondes at that toun,
Whil that the seege theraboute lay.
And yet now the olde Creon, weylaway!   80
That lord is now of Thebes the citee,
Fulfild of ire and of iniquitee,
He, for despit, and for his tirannye,
To do the dede bodies vileinye,
Of alle our lordes, whiche that been slawe,

---

[1] *Hg, etc.; El*, And.
[2] *Hg, etc.; El*, crye.

He hath alle the bodies on an heepe ydrawe,
And wol nat suffren hem, by noon assent,
Neither to been yburied nor ybrent,
But maketh houndes ete hem in despit.'
And with that word, withouten moore respit,   90
They fillen gruf, and criden pitously,
'Have on us wrecched wommen som mercy,
And lat our sorwe sinken in thin herte.'

  This gentil duk doun from his courser sterte
With herte pitous, whan he herde hem speke.
Him thoughte that his herte wolde breke,
Whan he saugh hem so pitous and so maat,
That whilom weren of so greet estaat.
And in his armes he hem alle up hente,
And hem conforteth in ful good entente;   100
And swoor his oth, as he was trewe knight,
He wolde doon so ferforthly his might
Upon the tiraunt Creon hem to wreke,
That al the peple of Grece sholde speke
How Creon was of Theseus yserved,
As he that hadde his deeth ful wel deserved.
And right anoon, withouten more abood,
His baner he desplayeth, and forth rood
To Thebesward, and al his hoost biside;
No neer Atthenes wolde he go ne ride,   110
Ne take his ese fully half a day,
But onward on his wey that night he lay;
And sente anon Ypolita the queene,
And Emelye, hir yonge suster sheene,
Unto the toun of Atthenes to dwelle;
And forth he rit; ther is namoore to telle.

The rede statue of Mars with spere and targe
So shineth in his white baner large,
That alle the feeldes gliteren up and doun;
And by his baner born is his penoun   120
Of gold ful riche, in which ther was ybete
The Minotaur which that he slough in Crete.
Thus rit this duk, thus rit this conquerour,
And in his hoost of chivalrye the flour,
Til that he cam to Thebes, and alighte
Faire in a feeld, ther as he thoughte fighte.
But, shortly for to speken of this thing,
With Creon, which that was of Thebes king,
He faught, and slough him manly as a knight
In plein bataille, and putte the folk to flight;   130
And by assaut he wan the citee after,
And rente adoun bothe wall, and sparre, and rafter;
And to the ladies he restored again
The bones of hir housbondes that weren slain,
To doon obsequies, as was tho the gise.
But it were al to long for to devise
The grete clamour and the waymentinge
That the ladies made at the brenninge
Of the bodies, and the grete honour
That Theseus, the noble conquerour,   140
Dooth to the ladies, whan they from him wente;
But shortly for to telle is min entente.
Whan that this worthy duk, this Theseus,
Hath Creon slain, and wonne Thebes thus,
Stille in that feeld he took al night his reste,
And dide with al the contree as him leste.
  To ransake in the taas of the bodies dede,

Hem for to strepe of harneis and of wede,
The pilours diden bisynesse and cure,
After the bataille and disconfiture.   150
And so bifel, that in the taas they founde,
Thurgh-girt with many a grevous blody wounde,
Two yonge knightes ligginge by and by,
Bothe in oon armes, wroght ful richely;
Of whiche two, Arcita highte that oon,
And that oother knight highte Palamon.
Nat fully quike, ne fully dede they were,
But by hir cote-armures, and by hir gere,
The heraudes knewe hem best in special,
As they that weren of the blood royal   160
Of Thebes, and of sustren two yborn.
Out of the taas the pilours han hem torn,
And han hem caried softe unto the tente
Of Theseus, and ful soone he hem sente
To Atthenes, to dwellen in prisoun
Perpetuelly, he nolde no raunsoun.
And whan this worthy duk hath thus ydon,
He took his hoost, and hoom he rood anon
With laurer crowned as a conquerour;
And there he liveth in joye and in honour   170
Terme of his lyve; what nedeth wordes mo?
And in a tour, in angwissh and in wo,
This Palamon, and his felawe Arcite,
For everemoore, ther may no gold hem quite.
        This passeth yeer by yeer, and day by day,
Til it fil ones, in a morwe of May,
That Emelye, that fairer was to sene
Than is the lilie upon his stalke grene,

And fressher than the May with floures newe—
For with the rose colour stroof hir hewe,   180
I noot which was the finer of hem two—
Er it were day, as was hir wone to do,
She was arisen, and al redy dight;
For May wol have no slogardrye anight.
The sesoun priketh every gentil herte,
And maketh him out of his sleep to sterte,
And seith, 'Aris, and do thin observaunce.'
This maked Emelye have remembraunce
To doon honour to May, and for to rise.
Yclothed was she fressh, for to devise.   190
Hir yelow heer was broided in a tresse,
Bihinde hir bak, a yerde long, I gesse.
And in the gardin, at the sonne upriste,
She walketh up and doun, and as hir liste
She gadereth floures, party white and rede,
To make a subtil gerland for hir hede,
And as an aungel hevenisshly she song.
The grete tour, that was so thicke and strong,
Which of the castel was the chief dongeoun,
(Ther as the knightes weren in prisoun,   200
Of which I tolde yow, and tellen shal)
Was evene joinant to the gardin wal,
Ther as this Emelye hadde hir pleyinge.
Bright was the sonne, and cleer that morweninge,
And[1] Palamon, this woful prisoner,
As was his wone, by leve of his gailer,
Was risen, and romed in a chambre an heigh,
In which he al the noble citee seigh,

[1] *El*, And this.

And eek the gardin, ful of braunches grene,
Ther as this fresshe Emelye the shene   210
Was in hir walk, and romed up and doun.
This sorweful prisoner, this Palamoun,
Goth in the chambre, rominge to and fro,
And to himself compleininge of his wo;
That he was born, ful ofte he seide, 'allas!'
And so bifel, by aventure or cas,
That thurgh a window, thicke of many a barre
Of iren, greet and square as any sparre,
He caste his eye upon Emelya,
And therwithal he bleinte, and cride, 'A!'   220
As though he stongen were unto the herte.
And with that cry Arcite anon upsterte,
And seide, 'Cosin min, what eileth thee,
That art so pale and deedly on to see?
Why cridestow? Who hath thee doon offence?
For Goddes love, taak al in pacience
Oure prisoun, for it may noon oother be;
Fortune hath yeven us this adversitee.
Som wicke aspect or disposicioun
Of Saturne, by sum constellacioun,   230
Hath yeven us this, although we hadde it sworn;
So stood the hevene whan that we were born;
We moste endure it[1]: this is the short and plain.'
    This Palamon answerde, and seide again,
'Cosin, for sothe, of this opinioun
Thou hast a vein imaginacioun.
This prison caused me nat for to crye,
But I was hurt right now thurghout min eye

---

[1] *El, om.* it.

Into min herte, that wol my bane be.
The fairnesse of that lady that I see 240
Yond in the gardin romen to and fro,
Is cause of al my crying and my wo.
I noot wher she be womman or goddesse;
But Venus is it, soothly, as I gesse.'
And therwithal on knees doun he fil,
And seide: 'Venus, if it be thy wil
Yow in this gardin thus to transfigure
Bifore me, sorweful wrecche creature,
Out of this prisoun help that we may scapen.
And if so be my destinee be shapen 250
By eterne word to dien in prisoun,
Of our linage have som compassioun,
That is so lowe ybroght by tirannye.'
And with that word Arcite gan espye
Wher as this lady romed to and fro.
And with that sighte hir beautee hurte him so,
That if that Palamon was wounded sore,
Arcite is hurt as muche as he, or moore.
And with a sigh he seide pitously:
'The fresshe beautee sleeth me sodeinly 260
Of hir that rometh in the yonder place;
And but I have hir mercy and hir grace,
That I may seen hir atte leeste weye,
I nam but deed; ther is namoore to seye.'
   This Palamon, whan he tho wordes herde,
Dispitously he looked, and answerde:
'Wheither seystow this in ernest, or in pley?
'Nay,' quod Arcite, 'in ernest, by my fey!
God help me so, me list ful yvele pleye.'

This Palamon gan knitte his browes tweye: 270
'It nere,' quod he, 'to thee no greet honour
For to be fals, ne for to be traitour
To me, that am thy cosin, and thy brother
Ysworn ful depe, and ech of us til oother,
That nevere, for to dien in the peine,
Til that deeth departe shal us tweine,
Neither of us in love to hindre oother,
Ne in noon oother cas, my leeve brother;
But that thou sholdest trewely forthren me
In every cas, as I shal forthren thee.   280
This was thin ooth, and min also, certein;
I wot right wel, thou darst it nat withseyn.
Thus artow of my conseil, out of doute.
And now thou woldest falsly been aboute
To love my lady, whom I love and serve,
And evere shal, til that min herte sterve.
Nay, certes, false Arcite, thou shalt nat so.
I loved hir first, and tolde thee my wo
As to my conseil, and to my brother sworn
To forthre me, as I have toold biforn.   290
For which thou art ybounden as a knight
To helpen me, if it lay in thy might,
Or elles artow fals, I dar wel seyn.'
This Arcite ful proudly spak agein:
'Thou shalt,' quod he, 'be rather fals than I;
And thou art fals, I telle thee outrely;
For paramour I loved hir first er thow.
What wiltow seyn? Thou woost[1] nat yet now
Wheither she be a womman or goddesse.

[1] *Hg*; *El*, wistest.

Thin is affeccioun of hoolynesse,   300
And min is love, as to a creature;
For which I tolde thee min aventure
As to my cosin, and my brother sworn.
I pose that thou lovedest hir biforn;
Wostow nat wel the olde clerkes sawe,
That 'who shal yeve a lovere any lawe?
Love is a gretter lawe, by my pan,
Than may be yeve of[1] any erthly man.'
And therfore positif lawe and swich decree
Is broken al day for love, in ech degree.   310
A man moot nedes love, maugree his heed.
He may nat flee it, thogh he sholde be deed,
Al be she maide, or widwe, or elles wif.
And eek it is nat likly, al thy lif,
To stonden in hir grace; namoore shal I;
For wel thou woost thyselven, verraily,
That thou and I be dampned to prisoun
Perpetuelly; us gaineth no raunsoun.
We striven, as dide the houndes for the boon,
They foughte al day, and yet hir part was noon;   320
Ther cam a kite, whil they weren so wrothe,
And baar awey the boon bitwixe hem bothe.
And therfore at the kinges court, my brother,
Ech man for himself, ther is noon oother.
Love if thee list; for I love and ay shal;
And soothly, leeve brother, this is al.
Heere in this prisoun moote we endure,
And everich of us take his aventure.'

    Greet was the strif, and long, bitwix hem tweye,

<hr>

[1] *Other MSS.*, to.

If that I hadde leiser for to seye;   330
But to th'effect. It happed on a day,
(To telle it yow as shortly as I may)
A worthy duk that highte Perotheus,
That felawe was to Duk Theseus
Sin thilke day that they were children lite,
Was come to Atthenes, his felawe to visite,
And for to pleye, as he was wont to do,
For in this world he loved no man so;
And he loved him as tendrely again.
So wel they loved, as olde bokes sayn,   340
That whan that oon was deed, soothly to telle,
His felawe wente and soughte him doun in helle;
But of that storye list me nat to write.
Duk Perotheus loved wel Arcite,
And hadde him knowe at Thebes yeer by yere;
And finally, at requeste and preyere
Of Perotheus, withouten any raunsoun,
Duk Theseus him leet out of prisoun,
Frely to goon, wher that him liste overal,
In swich a gise, as I you tellen shal.   350
This was the forward, pleinly for t'endite,
Bitwixen Theseus and him Arcite:
That if so were, that Arcite were yfounde
Evere in his lif, by day or night, o[1] stounde
In any contree of this Theseus,
And he were caught, it was acorded thus,
That with a swerd he sholde lese his heed;
Ther nas noon oother remedye ne reed,
But taketh his leve, and homward he him spedde;

[1] *El*, or *see note.*

Let him be war, his nekke lith to wedde.   360
    How greet a sorwe suffreth now Arcite!
The deeth he feeleth thurgh his herte smite;
He wepeth, waileth, crieth pitously;
To sleen himself he waiteth prively.
He seide, 'Allas that day that I¹ was born!
Now is my prisoun worse than biforn;
Now is me shape eternally to dwelle
Nat in my purgatorye, but in helle.
Allas that evere knew I Perotheus!
For elles hadde I dwelled with Theseus   370
Yfetered in his prisoun everemo.
Than hadde I been in blisse, and nat in wo.
Oonly the sighte of hir, whom that I serve,
Though that I nevere hir grace may deserve,
Wolde han suffised right ynough for me.
O dere cosin Palamon,' quod he,
'Thin is the victorye of this aventure,
Ful blisfully in prisoun maystow dure;
In prisoun? certes nay, but in paradis!
Wel hath Fortune yturned thee the dis,   380
That hast the sight of hir, and I th'absence.
For possible is, sin thou hast hir presence,
And art a knight, a worthy and an able,
That by² som cas, sin Fortune is chaungeable,
Thou mayst to thy desir somtime atteine.
But I, that am exiled, and bareine
Of alle grace, and in so greet dispeir,
That ther nis erthe, water, fir, ne eir,

---

¹ *El*, he.
² *El, om*, by.

Ne creature, that of hem maked is,
That may me heele or doon confort in this—   390
Wel oughte I sterve in wanhope and distresse.
Farwel my lif, my lust, and my gladnesse.
Allas, why pleinen folk so in commune
On purveiaunce of God, or of Fortune,
That yeveth hem ful ofte in many a gise
Wel bettre than they can hemself devise?
Som man desireth for to han richesse,
That cause is of his moerdre or greet siknesse.
And som man wolde out of his prison fain,
That in his hous is of his meinee slain.   400
Infinite harmes been in this mateere;
We witen nat what thing[1] we preyen here.
We faren as he that dronke is as a mous;
A dronke man woot wel that he hath an hous,
But he noot which the righte wey is thider;
And to a dronke man the wey is slider;
And certes, in this world so faren we;
We seken faste after felicitee,
But we goon wrong ful often, trewely.
Thus may we seyn alle, and namely I,   410
That wende and hadde a greet opinioun,
That I mighte escapen from prisoun,
Thanne hadde I been in joye and perfit heele,
Ther now I am exiled fro my wele.
Sin that I may nat seen yow, Emelye,
I nam but deed; ther nis no remedye.'
     Upon that oother side Palamon,
Whan that he wiste Arcite was agon,

[1] *El, om.* thing.

Swich sorwe he maketh, that the grete tour
Resouned of his youling and clamour.   420
The pure fettres on his shines grete
Weren of his bittre salte teeres wete.
'Allas!' quod he, 'Arcita, cosin min,
Of al our strif, God woot, the fruit is thin.
Thow walkest now in Thebes at thy large,
And of my wo thou yevest litel charge.
Thou mayst, sin thou hast wisdom and manhede,
Assemblen alle the folk of oure kinrede,
And make a werre so sharpe on this citee,
That by som aventure, or som tretee,   430
Thou mayst have hir to lady and to wif,
For whom that I moste nedes lese my lif.
For, as by wey of possibilitee,
Sith thou art at thy large, of prisoun free,
And art a lord, greet is thin avauntage,
Moore than is min, that sterve here in a cage.
For I moot wepe and waile, whil I live,
With al the wo that prison may me yeve,
And eek with peine that love me yeveth also,
That doubleth al my torment and my wo.'   440
Therwith the fir of jalousye upsterte
Withinne his brest, and hente him by the herte
So woodly, that he lik was to biholde
The box-tree, or the asshen dede and colde.
Thanne seide he: 'O crueel goddes, that governe
This world with binding of youre word eterne,
And writen in the table of atthamaunt
Youre parlement, and youre eterne graunt,
What is mankinde moore unto yow holde

Than is the sheep, that rouketh in the folde?   450
For slain is man right as another beest,
And dwelleth eek in prison and arreest,
And hath siknesse, and greet adversitee,
And ofte times giltlees, pardee.
What governance is in this prescience,
That giltlees tormenteth innocence?
And yet encresseth this al my penaunce,
That man is bounden to his observaunce,
For Goddes sake, to letten of his wille,
Ther as a beest may al his lust fulfille.   460
And whan a beest is deed, he hath no peine;
But after his deeth man moot wepe and pleine,
Though in this world he have care and wo:
Withouten doute it may stonden so.
The answere of this lete I to divinis,
But wel I woot, that in this world greet pine is.
Allas! I se a serpent or a theef,
That many a trewe man hath doon mescheef,
Goon at his large, and where him list may turne.
But I moot been in prisoun thurgh Saturne,   470
And eek thurgh Juno, jalous and eek wood,
That hath destroyed wel ny al the blood
Of Thebes, with hise waste walles wide.
And Venus sleeth me on that other side,
For jalousye, and fere of him Arcite.'
  Now wol I stynte of Palamon a lite,
And lete him in his prisoun stille dwelle,
And of Arcita forth I wol yow telle.
The somer¹ passeth, and the nightes longe

¹ *El*, sonne.

Encressen double wise the peines stronge 480
Bothe of the lovere and the prisoner.
I noot which hath the wofuller mester.
For shortly for to seyn, this Palamoun
Perpetuelly is dampned to prisoun,
In cheines and in fettres to been deed;
And Arcite is exiled upon his heed
For evere mo as out of that contree,
Ne nevere mo he shal his lady see.
Yow¹ loveres axe I now this questioun,
Who hath the worse, Arcite or Palamoun? 490
That oon may seen his lady day by day,
But in prison he moot dwelle alway.
That oother wher him list may ride or go,
But seen his lady shal he nevere mo.
Now demeth as yow list, ye that can,
For I wol telle forth as I bigan.

Explicit prima pars. Sequitur pars secunda

Whan that Arcite to Thebes comen was,
Ful ofte a day he swelte and seide 'allas,'
For seen his lady shal he nevere mo.
And shortly to concluden al his wo, 500
So muche sorwe hadde nevere creature
That is, or shal, whil that the world may dure.
His sleep, his mete, his drinke is him biraft,
That lene he wexeth, and drye as is a shaft.
His eyen holwe, and grisly to biholde;
His hewe falow, and pale as asshen colde,

¹ *El,* Now.

And solitarye he was, and evere allone,
And waillinge al the night, makinge his mone.
And if he herde song or instrument,
Then wolde he wepe, he mighte nat be stent;   510
So feble eek were hise spirits, and so lowe,
And chaunged so, that no man coude knowe
His speche nor his vois, though men it herde.
And in his geere, for al the world he ferde
Nat oonly lik the loveris maladye
Of hereos, but rather lik manie
Engendred of humour malencolic,
Biforne,[1] in his celle fantastic.
And shortly, turned was al up-so-doun
Bothe habit and eek disposicioun   520
Of him, this woful lovere daun Arcite.
What sholde I al day of his wo endite?
Whan he endured hadde a yeer or two
This crueel torment, and this peine and wo,
At Thebes, in his contree, as I seide,
Upon a night, in sleepe as he him leide,
Him thoughte how that the winged god Mercurye
Biforn him stood, and bad him to be murye.
His slepy yerde in hond he bar uprighte;
An hat he werede upon[2] hise heris brighte.   530
Arrayed was this god (as he[3] took keepe)
As he was whan that Argus took his sleepe;
And seide him thus: 'To Atthenes shaltou wende;
Ther is thee shapen of thy wo an ende.'
And with that word Arcite wook and sterte.

[1] *El*, Biforn his owene. *(See note.)*
[2] *El*, up.   [3] *El*, I.

'Now trewely, hou soore that me smerte,'
Quod he, 'to Atthenes right now wol I fare;
Ne for the drede of deeth shal I nat spare
To se my lady, that I love and serve;
In hir presence I recche nat to sterve.'   540
And with that word he caughte a greet mirour,
And saugh that chaunged was al his colour,
And saugh his visage al in another kinde.
And right anon it ran him in his minde,
That, sith his face was so disfigured
Of maladye, the which he hadde endured,
He mighte wel, if that he bar him lowe,
Live in Atthenes everemoore unknowe,
And seen his lady wel ny day by day.
And right anon he chaungede his array,   550
And cladde him as a poure laborer,
And al allone, save oonly a squier,
That knew his privetee and al his cas,
Which was disgised pourely, as he was,
To Atthenes is he goon the nexte way.
And to the court he wente upon a day,
And at the gate he profreth his servise,
To drugge and drawe, what so men wol devise.
And, shortly of this matere for to seyn,
He fil in office with a chamberlein,   560
The which that dwellinge was with Emelye.
For he was wis, and coude soon espye
Of every servaunt which that serveth here.
Wel coude he hewen wode, and water bere,
For he was yong and mighty for the nones,
And therto he was long and big of bones

To doon that any wight can him devise.
A yeer or two he was in this servise,
Page of the chambre of Emelye the brighte;
And 'Philostrate' he seide that he highte.   570
But half so wel biloved a man as he
Ne was ther nevere in court, of his degree;
He was so gentil of condicioun,
That thurghout al the court was his renoun.
They seiden that it were a charitee
That Theseus wolde enhauncen his degree,
And putten him in worshipful servise,
Ther as he mighte his vertu excercise.
And thus, withinne a while, his name is spronge
Bothe of hise dedes, and his goode tonge,   580
That Theseus hath taken him so neer
That of his chambre he made him a squier,
And gaf him gold to maintene his degree;
And eek men broghte him out of his contree
From yeer to yeer ful prively his rente;
But honestly and slyly he it spente,
That no man wondred how that he it hadde.
And thre yeer in this wise his lif he ladde,
And bar him so in pees and eek in werre,
Ther was no man that Theseus hath derre.   590
And in this blisse lete I now Arcite,
And speke I wol of Palamon a lite.
    In derknesse and horrible and strong prisoun
Thise seven yeer hath seten Palamoun,
Forpined, what for wo and for distresse;
Who feeleth double soor and hevynesse
But Palamon, that love destreineth so,

That wood out of his wit he goth for wo?
And eek therto he is a prisoner
Perpetuelly, noght oonly for a yer.   600
Who coude rime in Englissh proprely
His martyrdom? for sothe, it am nat I;
Therfore I passe as lightly as I may.
It fel that in the seventhe yer, in May,
The thridde night, (as olde bookes seyn,
That al this storye tellen moore plein,)
Were it by aventure or destinee,
(As, whan a thing is shapen, it shal be,)
That, soone after the midnight, Palamoun,
By helping of a freend, brak his prisoun,   610
And fleeth the citee faste as he may go,
For he hadde yeve his gailer drinke so
Of a clarree, maad of a certein win,
With[1] nercotikes and opie of Thebes fin,
That al that night, thogh that men wolde him shake,
The gailer sleepe, he mighte nat awake;
And thus he fleeth as faste as evere he may.
The night was short, and faste by the day,
That nedes cost he moot himselven hide,
And til a grove, faste ther biside,   620
With dredeful foot thanne stalketh Palamoun.
For shortly, this was his opinioun,
That in that grove he wolde him hide al day,
And in the night thanne wolde he take his way
To Thebesward, his freendes for to preye
On Theseus to helpe him to werreye;
And shortly, outher he wolde lese his lif,

[1] *El,* Cf.

Or winnen Emelye unto his wif;
This is th'effect and his entente plein.
    Now wol I turne to Arcite agein,   630
That litel wiste how ny that was his care,
Til that Fortune had broght him in the snare.
    The bisy larke, messager of day,
Salueth in hir song the morwe gray;
And firy Phebus riseth up so brighte,
That al the orient laugheth of the lighte,
And with hise stremes dryeth in the greves
The silver dropes hanginge on the leves.
And Arcita, that is in the court royal
With Theseus, his squier principal,   640
Is risen, and looketh on the mirye day.
And, for to doon his observaunce to May,
Remembringe on the point of his desir,
He on a courser, startlinge as the fir,
Is riden into the feeldes, him to pleye,
Out of the court, were it a mile or tweye;
And to the grove, of which that I yow tolde,
By aventure his wey he gan to holde,
To maken him a gerland of the greves,
Were it of wodebinde or hawethorn leves,   650
And loude he song ayein the sonne shene:
'May, with alle thy floures and thy grene,
Welcome be thou, faire fresshe May,
In hope that I som grene gete may.'
And from his courser, with a lusty herte,
Into the[1] grove ful hastily he sterte,
And in a path he rometh up and doun,

[1] *El*, a.

Ther as by aventure this Palamoun
Was in a bussh, that no man mighte him se,
For soore aferd of his deeth thanne was he.   660
Nothing ne knew he that it was Arcite:
God woot he wolde have trowed it ful lite.
But sooth is seid, go sithen many yeres,
That feeld hath eyen, and the wode hath eres.
It is ful fair a man to bere him evene,
For al day meeteth men at unset stevene.
Ful litel woot Arcite of his felawe,
That was so ny to herknen al his sawe,
For in the bussh he sitteth now ful stille.
  Whan that Arcite had romed al his fille,   670
And songen al the roundel lustily,
Into a studye he fil al sodeinly,
As doon thise loveres in hir queinte geres,
Now in the crope, now doun in the breres,
Now up, now doun, as boket in a welle.
Right as the Friday, soothly for to telle,
Now it shineth, now it reineth faste,
Right so can geery Venus overcaste
The hertes of hir folk; right as hir day
Is gereful, right so chaungeth she array;   680
Selde is the Friday al the wowke ylike.
Whan that Arcite had songe, he gan to sike,
And sette him doun withouten any moore:
'Allas!' quod he, 'that day that I was bore!
How longe, Juno, thurgh thy crueltee,
Woltow werreyen Thebes the citee?
Allas! ybroght is to confusioun
The blood royal of Cadme and Amphioun;

Of Cadmus, which that was the firste man
That Thebes bulte, or first the toun bigan,   690
And of the citee first was crouned king,
Of his linage am I, and his ofspring
By verray ligne, as of the stok royal:
And now I am so caitif and so thral,
That he, that is my mortal enemy,
I serve him as his squier pourely.
And yet dooth Juno me wel moore shame,
For I dar noght biknowe min owene name,
But ther as I was wont to highte Arcite,
Now highte I Philostrate, noght worth a mite.   700
Allas! thou felle Mars, allas! Juno,
Thus hath your ire our kinrede al fordo,
Save oonly me, and wrecched Palamoun,
That Theseus martyreth in prisoun.
And over al this, to sleen me outrely,
Love hath his firy dart so brenningly
Ystiked thurgh my trewe, careful herte,
That shapen was my deeth erst than my sherte.
Ye sleen me with youre eyen, Emelye;
Ye been the cause wherfor that I die.   710
Of al the remenant of min oother care
Ne sette I nat the montaunce of a tare,
So that I coude doon aught to your plesaunce.'
And with that word he fil doun in a traunce
A longe time; and after he upsterte.
    This Palamoun, that thoughte that thurgh his herte
He felt a coold swerd sodeinliche glide,
For ire he quook, no lenger wolde he bide.
And whan that he had herd Arcites tale,

As he were wood, with face deed and pale,   720
He stirte him up out of the buskes thicke,
And seide: 'Arcite, false traitour wicke,
Now artow hent, that lovest my lady so,
For whom that I have al this peine and wo,
And art my blood and to my conseil sworn,
As I ful ofte have seid thee heer-biforn,
And hast bijaped heere Duk Theseus,
And falsly chaunged hast thy name thus;
I wol be deed, or elles thou shalt die.
Thou shalt nat love my lady Emelye,   730
But I wol love hir oonly, and namo;
For I am Palamon, thy mortal foo.
And though that I no wepene have in this place,
But out of prison am astert by grace,
I drede noght that outher thou shalt die,
Or thou shalt nat loven Emelye.
Chees which thou wolt, or thou shalt nat asterte.'
This Arcite, with ful despitous herte,
Whan he him knew, and hadde his tale herd,
As fiers as leoun pulled out his swerd,   740
And seide thus: 'by God that sit above,
Nere it that thou art sik and wood for love,
And eek that thou no wepne hast in this place,
Thou sholdest nevere out of this grove pace,
That thou ne sholdest dien of min hond.
For I defye the seuretee and the bond
Which that thou seyst that I have maad to thee.
What, verray fool, think wel that love is free,
And I wol love hir, maugree al thy might!
But, for as much thou art a worthy knight,   750

And wilnest to darreine hire by bataille,
Have heer my trouthe, tomorwe I wol nat faille,
Withoute witing of any oother wight,
That heere I wol be founden as a knight,
And bringen harneis right ynough for thee;
And chees the beste, and leve the worste for me.
And mete and drinke this night wol I bringe
Ynough for thee, and clothes for thy beddinge.
And, if so be that thou my lady winne,
And sle me in this wode ther I am inne,   760
Thou mayst wel have thy lady, as for me.'
This Palamon answerde: 'I graunte it thee.'
And thus they been departed til amorwe,
Whan ech of hem had leid his feith to borwe.
  O Cupide, out of alle charitee!
O regne, that wolt no felawe have with thee!
Ful sooth is seid, that love ne lordshipe
Wol noght, hir thankes, have no felaweshipe.
Wel finden that Arcite and Palamoun.
Arcite is riden anon unto the toun,   770
And on the morwe, er it were dayes light,
Ful prively two harneis hath he dight,
Bothe suffisaunt and mete to darreine
The bataille in the feeld bitwix hem tweine.
And on his hors, allone as he was born,
He carieth al the harneis him biforn;
And in the grove, at time and place yset,
This Arcite and this Palamon ben met.
To chaungen gan the colour in hir face,
Right as the hunters in the regne of Trace,   780
That stondeth[1] at the gappe with a spere,

---

[1] *Hg*, stonden.

Whan hunted is the leoun and the bere,
And hereth him come russhing in the greves,
And breketh bothe bowes and the leves,
And thinketh, 'heere cometh my mortal enemy,
Withoute faille, he moot be deed, or I;
For outher I moot sleen him at the gappe,
Or he moot sleen me, if that me mishappe':
So ferden they, in chaunging of hir hewe,
As fer as everich of hem oother knewe.   790
Ther nas no 'Good day,' ne no saluing;
But streight, withouten word or rehersing,
Everich of hem heelp for to armen oother,
As freendly as he were his owene brother;
And after that, with sharpe speres stronge
They foinen ech at oother wonder longe.
Thou mightest wene that this Palamoun
In his fighting were as[1] a wood leoun;
And as a crueel tigre was Arcite.
As wilde bores gonne they to smite,   800
That frothen whit as foom for ire wood.
Up to the anclee foghte they in hir blood.
And in this wise I lete hem fighting dwelle,
And forth I wole of Theseus yow telle.

   The destinee, ministre general,
That executeth in the world overal
The purveiaunce, that God hath seyn biforn,
So strong it is, that though the world had sworn
The contrarye of a thing, by ye or nay,
Yet somtime it shal fallen on a day   810
That falleth nat eft withinne a thousand yeere.
For certeinly oure appetites heere,

---

[1] *El, om.* as.

Be it of werre, or pees, or hate, or love,
Al is this reuled by the sighte above.
This mene I now by mighty Theseus,
That for to hunten is so desirus,
And namely at the grete hert in May,
That in his bed ther daweth him no day
That he nis clad, and redy for to ride
With hunte and horn, and houndes him biside.   820
For in his hunting hath he swich delit,
That it is al his joye and appetit
To been himself the grete hertes bane,
For after Mars he serveth now Diane.

   Cleer was the day, as I have toold er this,
And Theseus, with alle joye and blis,
With his Ypolita, the faire queene,
And Emelye, clothed al in grene,
On hunting be they riden royally.
And to the grove, that stood ful faste by,   830
In which ther was an hert, as men him tolde,
Duk Theseus the streighte wey hath holde.
And to the launde he rideth him ful right,
For thider was the hert wont have his flight,
And over a brook, and so forth in his weye.
This duk wol han a cours at him or tweye
With houndes, swiche as him list comaunde.
And whan this duk was come unto the launde,
Under the sonne he looketh, and anon
He was war of Arcite and Palamon,   840
That foughten breme, as it were bores two;
The brighte swerdes wenten to and fro
So hidously, that with the leeste strook

It semed as it wolde felle[1] an ook;
But what they were, nothing he ne woot.
This duk his courser with his spores smoot,
And at a stert he was bitwix hem two,
And pullede out a swerd and cride, 'Hoo!
Namoore, upon peine of lesinge of youre heed.
By mighty Mars, he shal anon be deed   850
That smiteth any strook, that I may seen!
But telleth me what mystiers men ye been,
That been so hardy for to fighten heere
Withouten juge or oother officere,
As it were in a listes, royally?'
This Palamon answerde hastily,
And seide, 'Sire, what nedeth wordes mo?
We have the deeth disserved bothe two.
Two woful wrecches been we, two caitives,
That been encombred of oure owene lives;   860
And as thou art a rightful lord and juge,
Ne yeve us neither mercy ne refuge.
But sle me first, for seinte charitee;
But sle my felawe eek as wel as me.
Or sle him first; for, though thou knowest it lite,
This is thy mortal foo, this is Arcite,
That fro thy lond is banisshed on his heed,
For which he hath deserved to be deed.
For this is he that cam unto thy gate,
And seide that he highte Philostrate.   870
Thus hath he japed thee ful many a yer,
And thou hast maked him thy chief squier.
And this is he that loveth Emelye:

[1] *El*, fille.

For sith the day is come that I shal die,
I make pleinly my confessioun,
That I am thilke woful Palamoun
That hath thy prisoun broken wickedly.
I am thy mortal foo, and it am I
That loveth so hoote Emelye the brighte,
That I wol die present in hir sighte.   880
Wherfore I axe deeth and my juwise;
But sle my felawe in the same wise,
For bothe han we deserved to be slain.'

    This worthy duk answerde anon again,
And seide, 'This is a short conclusioun:
Youre owene mouth, by youre confessioun,
Hath dampned yow, and I wol it recorde,
It nedeth noght to pine yow with the corde.
Ye shal be deed, by mighty Mars the rede!'
The queene anon, for verray wommanhede   890
Gan for to wepe, and so dide Emelye,
And alle the ladies in the compaignye.
Greet pitee was it, as it thoughte hem alle,
That evere swich a chaunce sholde falle;
For gentil men they were, of greet estaat,
And nothing but for love was this debaat;
And sawe hir bloody woundes wide and soore;
And alle crieden, bothe lasse and moore,
'Have mercy, lord, upon us wommen alle!'
And on hir bare knees adoun they falle,   900
And wolde have kist his feet ther as he stood,
Til at the laste aslaked was his mood;
For pitee renneth soone in gentil herte.
And though he first for ire quook and sterte,

He hath considered shortly, in a clause,
The trespas of hem bothe, and eek the cause;
And although that his ire hir gilt accused,
Yet in his resoun he hem bothe excused,
As thus; he thoghte wel, that every man
Wol helpe himself in love, if that he can,   910
And eek delivere himself out of prisoun;
And eek his herte hadde compassioun
Of wommen, for they wepen[1] evere in oon;
And in his gentil herte he thoughte anon,
And softe unto himself he seide, 'Fy
Upon a lord that wol have no mercy,
But been a leoun, bothe in word and dede,
To hem that been in repentaunce and drede,
As wel as to a proud despitous man,
That wol maintene that he first bigan.   920
That lord hath litel of discrecioun,
That in swich cas can no divisioun,
But weyeth pride and humblesse after oon.'
And shortly, whan his ire is thus agoon,
He gan to looken up with eyen lighte,
And spak thise same wordes al on highte:
'The god of love, a! *benedicite*,
How mighty and how greet a lord is he!
Ayeins his might ther gaineth none obstacles,
He may be cleped a god for hise miracles;   930
For he can maken, at his owene gise,
Of everich herte as that him list divise.
Lo heere, this Arcite and this Palamoun,
That quitly weren out of my prisoun,

[1] *Hg,* wepten.

And mighte han lived in Thebes royally,
And witen I am hir mortal enemy,
And that hir deth lith in my might also,
And yet hath love, maugree hir eyen two,
Ibroght hem hider bothe for to die!
Now looketh, is nat that an heigh folye? 940
Who may ben a fool, but if he love?
Bihoold, for Goddes sake that sit above,
Se how they blede! be they noght wel arrayed?
Thus hath hir lord, the god of love, ypaid
Hir wages and hir fees for hir servise!
And yet they wenen for to been ful wise
That serven love, for aught that may bifalle!
But this is yet the beste game of alle,
That she, for whom they han this jolitee,
Can hem therfore as muche thank as me; 950
She woot namore of al this hoote fare,
By God, than woot a cockow or[1] an hare!
But al moot ben assayed, hoot and cold;
A man moot ben a fool, or yong or oold:
I woot it by myself ful yore agoon:
For in my time a servant was I oon.
And therfore, sin I knowe of loves peine,
And woot how sore it can a man distreine,
As he that hath ben caught ofte in his laas,
I yow foryeve al hoolly this trespaas, 960
At requeste of the queene that kneleth heere,
And eek of Emelye, my suster deere.
And ye shul bothe anon unto me swere,
That nevere mo ye shul my contree dere,

---

[1] *El, Hg, Cp*, of.

Ne make werre upon me night ne day,
But been my freendes in al that ye may;
I yow foryeve this trespas every del.'
And they him sworen his axing faire and wel,
And him of lordshipe and of mercy preyde,
And he hem graunteth grace, and thus he seide: 970
  'To speke of royal linage and richesse,
Though that she were a queene or a princesse,
Ech of yow bothe is worthy, doutelees,
To wedden whan time is, but nathelees[1]
I speke as for my suster Emelye,
For whom ye have this strif and jalousye.
Ye woot yourself she may not wedden two
At ones, though ye fighten everemo:
That oon of yow, al be him looth or lief,
He moot pipen in an ivy leef; 980
This is to seyn, she may nat now han bothe,
Al be ye nevere so jalouse, ne so wrothe.
And forthy I yow putte in this degree,
That ech of yow shal have his destinee
As him is shape; and herkneth in what wise;
Lo, heere youre ende of that I shal devise.
My wil is this, for plat conclusioun,
Withouten any replicacioun—
If that yow liketh, tak it for the beste:
That everich of yow shal goon wher him leste 990
Frely, withouten raunsoun or daunger;
And this day fifty wikes, fer ne ner,
Everich of yow shal bringe an hundred knightes,
Armed for listes up at alle rightes,

[1] *El*, is doutelees.

Al redy to darreine hir by bataille.
And this bihote I yow withouten faille
Upon my trouthe, and as I am a knight,
That wheither of yow bothe that hath might,
This is to seyn, that wheither he or thou
May with his hundred, as I spak of now,   1000
Sleen his contrarye, or out of listes drive,
Thanne shal I yeve Emelya to wive,
To whom that Fortune yeveth so fair a grace.
The listes shal I maken in this place,
And God so wisly on my soule rewe,
As I shall evene juge been and trewe.
Ye shul non oother ende with me maken,
That oon of yow ne shal be deed or taken.
And if yow thinketh this is wel ysaid,
Seyeth youre avis, and holdeth yow apaid.   1010
This is youre ende and youre conclusioun.'

Who looketh lightly now but Palamoun?
Who springeth up for joye but Arcite?
Who couthe telle, or who couthe it[1] endite,
The joye that is maked in the place
Whan Theseus hath doon so fair a grace?
But doun on knees wente every maner wight,
And thonken him with al hir herte and might,
And namely the Thebans often sithe.
And thus with good hope and with herte blithe 1020
They take hir leve, and homward gonne they ride
To Thebes, with hise olde walles wide.

[1] El, Gg, *om*. it.

Explicit secunda pars. Sequitur pars tercia

I trowe men wolde deme it necligence,
If I foryete to tellen the dispence
Of Theseus, that goth so bisily
To maken up the listes royally;
That swich a noble theatre as it was,
I dar wel seyn in this world ther nas.
The circuit a mile was aboute,
Walled of stoon, and diched al withoute.   1030
Round was the shape, in manere of compas,
Ful of degrees, the heighte of sixty pas,
That, whan a man was set on o degree,
He lette nat his felawe for to see.
    Estward ther stood a gate of marbul whit,
Westward, right swich another in the opposit.
And shortly to concluden, swich a place
Was noon in erthe, as in so litel space;
For in the lond ther was no crafty man
That geometrye or ars metric can,   1040
Ne portreitour, ne cervere of images,
That Theseus ne yaf mete and wages
The theatre for to maken and devise.
And for to doon his rite and sacrifise,
He estward hath upon the gate above,
In worshipe of Venus, goddesse of love,
Doon make an auter and an oratorie;
And on the gate westward, in memorye[1]
Of Mars, he maked hath right swich another,
That coste largely of gold a fother.   1050

[1] *El, Hg, Gg,* And on the westward, in memorye (see note).

And northward, in a touret on the wal,
Of alabastre whit and reed coral,
An oratorye, riche for to see,
In worshipe of Diane of chastitee,
Hath Theseus doon wroght in noble wise.
But yet hadde I foryeten to devise
The noble cerving, and the portreitures,
The shape, the contenaunce, and the figures,
That weren in thise oratories thre:
    First in the temple of Venus maystow se,   1060
Wroght on the wal, ful pitous to biholde,
The broken slepes and the sikes colde;
The sacred teres, and the waymentinge;
The firy strokes of [1] the desiringe,
That loves servants in this lif enduren;
The othes that hir covenants assuren;
Plesaunce and Hope, Desir, Fool-hardinesse,
Beautee and Youthe, Bauderye, Richesse,
Charmes and Force, Lesinges, Flaterye,
Despense, Bisynesse, and Jalousye,   1070
That wered of yelewe gooldes a gerland,
And a cockow sittinge on hir hand;
Festes, instruments, caroles, daunces,
Lust and array, and alle the circumstaunces
Of love, whiche that I rekned and rekne shal,[2]
By ordre weren peinted on the wal,
And mo than I can make of mencioun.
For soothly al the mount of Citheroun,
Ther Venus hath hir principal dwellinge

[1] El, and.
[2] Hg; El, rekned have and.

Was shewed on the wal in portreyinge,   1080
With al the gardin, and the lustinesse.
Nat was foryeten the porter Idelnesse,
Ne Narcisus the faire, of yore agon,
Ne[1] yet the folye of king Salomon,
Ne[2] eek the grete strengthe of Ercules,
Th'enchauntements of Medea and Circes,
Ne of Turnus, with the hardy fiers corage,
The riche Cresus, caitif in servage.
Thus may ye seen that wisdom ne richesse,
Beautee ne sleighte, strengthe, hardinesse,   1090
Ne may with Venus holde champartye;
For as hir list the world than may she gye.
Lo, alle thise folk so caught were in hir las,
Til they for wo ful ofte seide 'allas!'
Sufficeth heere ensamples oon or two,
And though I coude rekne a thousand mo.
  The statue of Venus, glorious for to se,
Was naked fletinge in the large see,
And fro the navele doun al covered was
With wawes grene, and brighte as any glas.   1100
A citole in hir right hand hadde she,
And on hir heed, ful semely for to se,
A rose gerland, fressh and wel smellinge;
Above hir heed hir dowves flikeringe.
Biforn hire stood hir sone Cupido,
Upon his shuldres winges hadde he two;
And blind he was, as it is ofte seene;
A bowe he bar, and arwes brighte and kene.
  Why sholde I noght as wel eek telle yow al

_1 El_, And.   _2 El_, And.

The portreiture, that was upon the wal   1110
Withinne the temple of mighty Mars the rede?
Al peinted was the wal, in lengthe and brede,
Lik to the estres of the grisly place,
That highte the grete temple of Mars in Trace,
In thilke colde frosty regioun,
Ther as Mars hath his soverein mansioun.

First on the wal was peinted a forest,
In which ther dwelleth neither man ne best,
With knotty knarry bareine trees olde
Of stubbes sharpe and hidouse to biholde;   1120
In which ther ran a rumbel and a swough,
As though a storm sholde bresten every bough:
And dounward from an hille, under a bente,
Ther stood the temple of Mars armipotente,
Wroght al of burned steel, of which the entree
Was long and streit, and gastly for to see.
And therout cam a rage and swich a vese,
That it made al the gate for to rese.
The northren light in at the dores shoon,
For windowe on the wal ne was ther noon,   1130
Thurgh which men mighten any light discerne.
The dore was al of adamant eterne,
Yclenched overthwart and endelong
With iren tough; and, for to make it strong,
Every piler, the temple to sustene,
Was tonne-greet, of iren bright and shene.

Ther saugh I first the dirke imagining
Of Felonye, and the compassing;
The crueel Ire, reed as any gleede;
The pikepurs, and the pale Drede;   1140

The smilere with the knife under the cloke;
The shepne brenninge, with the blake smoke;
The tresoun of the mordringe in the bedde;
The open werre, with woundes al bibledde;
Contek, with blody knife, and sharp manace;
Al ful of chirking was that sory place.
The sleere of himself yet saugh I ther,
His herte-blood hath bathed al his heer;
The nail ydriven in the shode anight;
The colde deeth, with mouth gaping upright.   1150
Amiddes of he temple sat Meschaunce,
With disconfort and sory contenaunce.
Yet saugh I Woodnesse laughinge in his rage;
Armed compleint, outhees, and fiers outrage.
The careine in the bussh, with throte ycorve:
A thousand slain, and nat oon of qualm ystorve;
The tiraunt, with the pray by force yraft;
The toun destroyed, ther was nothing laft.
Yet saugh I brent the shippes hoppesteres;
The hunte strangled with the wilde beres;   1160
The sowe freten the child right in the cradel;
The cook yscalded, for al his longe ladel.
Noght was foryeten by the infortune of Marte;
The cartere overriden with his carte,
Under the wheel ful lowe he lay adoun.
Ther were also, of Martes divisioun,
The barbour[1], and the bocher, and the smith,
That forgeth sharpe swerdes on his stith.
And al above, depeinted in a tour,
Saw I Conquest sittinge in greet honour,   1170

---

[1] *El*, laborer.

With the sharpe swerd over his heed
Hanginge by a soutil twines threed.
Depeinted was the slaughtre of Julius,
Of grete Nero, and of Antonius;
Al be that thilke time they were unborn,
Yet was hir deeth depeinted therbiforn,
By manasinge of Mars, right by figure;
So was it shewed in that portreiture
As is depeinted in the sterres[1] above
Who shal be slain or elles deed for love.   1180
Sufficeth oon ensample in stories olde,
I may not rekene hem alle, though I wolde.

    The statue of Mars upon a carte stood,
Armed, and looked grim as he were wood;
And over his heed ther shinen two figures
Of sterres, that been cleped in scriptures
That oon Puella, that oother Rubeus.
This god of armes was arrayed thus:
A wolf ther stood biforn him at his feet,
With eyen rede, and of a man he eet;   1190
With soutil pencel was depeinted this storye,
In redoutinge of Mars and of his glorye.

    Now to the temple of Diane the chaste
As shortly as I can I wol me haste,
To telle yow al the descripsioun
Depeinted been the walles up and doun
Of hunting and of shamefast chastitee.
Ther saugh I how woful Calistopee,
Whan that Diane agreved was with here,
Was turned from a womman til a bere,   1200

----

[1] *El*, certres.

And after was she maad the loode-sterre;
Thus was it peinted, I can say yow no ferre;
Hir sone is eek a sterre, as men may see.
Ther saugh I Dane, yturned til a tree,
I mene nat the goddesse Diane,
But Penneus doghter, which that highte Dane.
Ther saugh I Attheon an hert ymaked,
For vengeaunce that he saugh Diane al naked;
I saugh how that hise houndes have him caught,
And freeten him, for that they knewe him naught. 1210
Yet peinted was a litel forthermoor,
How Atthalante hunted the wilde boor,
And Meleagree, and many another mo,
For which Diane wroghte him care and wo.
Ther saugh I many another wonder storye,
The whiche me list nat drawen to memorye.
This goddesse on an hert ful¹ hye seet,
With smale houndes all aboute hir feet,
And undernethe hir feet she hadde a moone;
Wexing it was, and sholde wanie soone.   1220
In gaude grene hir statue clothed was,
With bowe in honde, and arwes in a cas.
Hir eyen caste she ful lowe adoun,
Ther Pluto hath his derke regioun.
A womman travaillinge was hir biforn,
But, for hir child so longe was unborn,
Ful pitously Lucina gan she calle,
And seide, 'Help, for thou mayst best of alle.'
Wel coude he peinten lifly that it wroghte,
With many a florin he the hewes boghte.   1230

¹ *El*, ful wel.

Now been the listes maad, and Theseus,
That at his grete cost arrayed thus
The temples and the theatre every deel,
Whan it was doon, him liked wonder weel.
But stinte I wol of Theseus a lite,
And speke of Palamon and of Arcite.

The day approcheth of hir retourninge,
That everich sholde an hundred knightes bringe,
The bataille to darreine, as I yow tolde;
And til Atthenes, hir covenants for to holde,   1240
Hath everich of hem broght an hundred knightes
Wel armed for the werre at alle rightes.
And sikerly, ther trowed many a man
That nevere, sithen that the world bigan,
As for to speke of knighthod of hir hond,
As fer as God hath maked see or lond,
Nas, of so fewe, so noble a compaignye.
For every wight that loved chivalrye,
And wolde, his thankes, han a passant name,
Hath preyd that he mighte ben of that game;   1250
And wel was him that therto chosen was.
For if ther fille tomorwe swich a cas,
Ye knowen wel that every lusty knight,
That loveth paramours, and hath his might,
Were it in Engelond, or elleswhere,
They wolde, hir thankes, wilnen to be there,
To fighte for a lady, *benedicite*!
It were a lusty sighte for to see.
And right so ferden they with Palamon.
With him ther wenten knightes many on;   1260
Som wol ben armed in an habergeoun,

And in a[1] brest-plat and a light[2] gipoun;
And somme woln have a paire plates large;
And somme woln have a Pruce sheeld, or a targe;
Somme woln been armed on hir legges weel,
And have an ax, and somme a mace of steel;
Ther is no newe gise that it nas old.
Armed were they, as I have you told,
Everich after his opinioun.

Ther maystow seen cominge with Palamon   1270
Ligurge himself, the grete king of Trace;
Blak was his berd, and manly was his face.
The cercles of his eyen in his heed,
They gloweden bitwixen yelow and reed;
And lik a grifphon looked he aboute,
With kempe heeris on his browes stoute;
His limes grete, his brawnes harde and stronge,
His shuldres brode, his armes rounde and longe;
And, as the gise was in his contree,
Ful hye upon a chaar of gold stood he,   1280
With foure white boles in the trais.
Instede of cote-armure over his harnais,
With nailes yelewe, and brighte as any gold,
He hadde a beres skin, col-blak, for-old.
His longe heer was cembd bihinde his bak,
As any ravenes fethere it shoon for-blak.
A wrethe of gold, arm-greet, of huge wighte,
Upon his heed, set ful of stones brighte,
Of fine rubies and of diamaunts.
Aboute his chaar ther wenten white alaunts,   1290
Twenty and mo, as grete as any steer,

---

[1] *El*, And in.   [2] *Almost all MSS.*, and in a light.

To hunten at the leoun or the deer,
And folwed him, with mosel faste ybounde,
Colered[1] of golde, and tourettes filed rounde.
An hundred lordes hadde he in his route
Armed ful wel, with hertes stierne and stoute.

With Arcite, in stories as men finde,
The grete Emetreus, the king of Inde,
Upon a steede bay, trapped in steel,
Covered in clooth of gold diapred weel,   1300
Cam ridinge lik the god of armes, Mars.
His cote-armure was of clooth of Tars,
Couched with perles white and rounde and grete.
His sadel was of brend gold newe ybete;
A mantel[2] upon his shulder hanginge,
Bratful of rubies reede, as fir sparklinge.
His crispe heer lik ringes was yronne,
And that was yelow, and glitered as the sonne.
His nose was heigh, his eyen bright citrin,
His lippes rounde, his colour was sangwin,   1310
A few frakenes in his face yspreind,
Betwixen yelow and somdel blak ymeind,
And as a leoun he his looking caste.
Of five and twenty yeer his age, I caste.
His berd was wel bigonne for to springe;
His vois was as a trompe thondringe.
Upon his heed he wered of laurer grene
A gerland fressh and lusty for to sene.
Upon his hand he bar, for his deduit,
An egle tame, as any lilye whit.   1320
An hundred lordes hadde he with him there,

---

[1] *Cp*, coleres.   [2] *Hg, Cp*, mantelet.

Al armed, save hir heddes, in al hir gere,
Ful richely in alle maner thinges.
For trusteth wel that dukes, erles, kinges,
Were gadered in this noble compaignye,
For love, and for encrees of chivalrye.
Aboute this king ther ran on every part
Ful many a tame leoun and leopard.
And in this wise thise lordes, alle and some,
Been on the Sonday to the citee come   1330
Aboute prime, and in the toun alight.

    This Theseus, this duk, this worthy knight,
Whan he had broght hem into his citee,
And inned hem, everich in his degree,
He festeth hem, and doth so greet labour
To esen hem, and doon hem al honour,
That yet men weneth that no maner wit
Of noon estaat ne coude amenden it.
The minstralcye, the service at the feeste,
The grete yiftes to the meeste and leeste,   1340
The riche array of Theseus paleis,
Ne who sat first ne last upon the deis,
What ladyes fairest been or best daunsinge,
Or which of hem can dauncen best and singe,
Ne who moost felingly speketh of love:
What haukes sitten on the perche above,
What houndes liggen in the floor adoun:
Of al this make I now no mencioun;
But al th'effect, that thinketh me the beste;
Now comth the point, and herkneth if yow leste.

    The Sonday night, er day bigan to springe,   1351
When Palamon the larke herde singe,

(Although it nere nat day by houres two,
Yet song the larke) and Palamon right tho[1]
With hooly herte, and with an heigh corage,
He roos, to wenden on his pilgrimage
Unto the blisful Citherea benigne,
I mene Venus, honurable and digne.
And in hir houre he walketh forth a pas
Unto the listes, ther hir temple was,   1360
And doun he kneleth, and with humble cheere
And herte soor, and seide in this manere:
   'Faireste of faire, o lady min Venus,
Doughter to Jove, and spouse of Vulcanus,
Thou gladere of the mount of Citheron,
For thilke love thou haddest to Adoon,
Have pitee of my bittre teeris smerte,
And taak min humble preyere at thin herte.
Allas! I ne have no langage to telle
Th'effectes ne the torments of min helle;   1370
Min herte may mine harmes nat biwreye;
I am so confus, that I can noght seye
But 'Mercy,' lady bright, that knowest weele
My thought, and seest what harmes that I feele.
Considere al this, and rewe upon my soore,
As wisly as I shal for evermoore,
Emforth my might, thy trewe servant be,
And holden werre alwey with chastitee—
That make I min avow, so ye me helpe.
I kepe noght of armes for to yelpe,   1380
Ne I ne axe nat tomorwe to have victorye,
Ne renoun in this cas, ne veine glorye

       [1] *Hg, Cp, etc.; El.* also.

Of pris of armes blowen up and doun,
But I wolde have fully possessioun
Of Emelye, and die in thy servise;
Find thow the manere hou, and in what wise.
I recche nat, but it may bettre be,
To have victorye of hem, or they of me,
So that I have my lady in mine armes.
For though so be that Mars is god of armes,   1390
Your vertu is so greet in hevene above,
That if yow list I shal wel have my love.
Thy temple wol I worshipe everemo,
And on thin auter, wher I ride or go,
I wol doon sacrifice, and fires beete.
And if ye wol nat so, my lady sweete,
Than preye I thee, tomorwe with a spere
That Arcita me thurgh the herte bere.
Thanne recke I noght, whan I have lost my lif,
Though that Arcita winne hir to his wif.   1400
This is th'effect and ende of my preyere:
Yif me my love, thou blisful lady deere.'
Whan the orison was doon of Palamon,
His sacrifice he dide, and that anon
Ful pitously, with alle circumstaunce,
Al telle I noght as now his observaunce.
But atte laste the statue of Venus shook,
And made a signe, wherby that he took
That his preyere accepted was that day.
For thogh the signe shewed a delay,   1410
Yet wiste he wel that graunted was his boone;
And with glad herte he wente him hoom ful soone.
    The thridde houre inequal that Palamon

Bigan to Venus temple for to gon,
Up roos the sonne, and up roos Emelye,
And to the temple of Diane gan hye.
Hir maidens, that she thider with hir ladde,
Ful redily with hem the fir they hadde,
Th'encens, the clothes, and the remenant al
That to the sacrifice longen shal;   1420
The hornes fulle of meeth, as was the gise;
Ther lakked noght to doon hir sacrifise,
Smokinge the temple, ful of clothes faire.
This Emelye, with herte debonaire,
Hir body wessh with water of a welle;
But how she dide hir rite I dar nat telle,
But it be any thing in general;
And yet it were a game to heeren al;
To him that meneth wel, it were no charge—
But it is good a man ben at his large.   1430
Hir brighte heer was cembd, untressed al;
A coroune of a grene ook cerial
Upon hir heed was set ful fair and meete.
Two fires on the auter gan she beete,
And dide hir thinges, as men may biholde
In Stace of Thebes, and thise bookes olde.
Whan kindled was the fir, with pitous chere
Unto Diane she spak, as ye may heere:
    'O chaste goddesse of the wodes grene,
To whom bothe hevene and erthe and see is sene,
Queene of the regne of Pluto derk and lowe,   1441
Goddesse of maidens, that min herte hast knowe
Ful many a yeer, and woost what I desire,
As keep me fro thy vengeaunce and thin ire,

That Attheon aboughte cruelly.
Chaste goddesse, wel wostow that I
Desire to been a maiden al my lif,
Ne nevere wol I be no love ne wif.
I am, thou woost, yet of thy compaignye,
A maide, and love huntinge and venerye,   1450
And for to walken in the wodes wilde,
And noght to been a wif, and be with childe.
Nought wol I knowe the compaignye of man.
Now help me, lady, sith ye may and can,
For tho thre formes that thou hast in thee.
And Palamon, that hath swich love to me,
And eek Arcite, that loveth me so soore,
This grace I preye thee withoute moore,
As¹ sende love and pees bitwixe hem two;
And fro me turne awey hir hertes so,   1460
That al hir hoote love, and hir desir,
And al hir bisy torment, and hir fir
Be queint, or turned in another place;
And if so be thou wolt do me no grace,
Or² if my destinee be shapen so,
That I shal nedes have oon of hem two,
As sende me him that moost desireth me.
Bihoold, goddesse of clene chastitee,
The bittre teeris that on my chekes falle.
Sin thou art maide, and kepere of us alle,   1470
My maidenhede thou kepe and wel conserve,
And whil I live a maide, I wol thee serve.'
    The fires brenne upon the auter cleere,
Whil Emelye was thus in hir preyere;

    ¹ *Hg*; *El*, *etc.*, And.   ² *El*, And

But sodeinly she saugh a sighte queinte,
For right anon oon of the fires queinte,
And quiked again, and after that anon
That oother fir was queint, and al agon;
And as it queinte it made a whistlinge,
As doon thise wete brondes in hir brenninge,   1480
And at the brondes ende out-ran anoon
As it were blody dropes many oon;
For which so soore agast was Emelye,
That she was wel ny mad, and gan to crye,
For she ne wiste what it signified;
But oonly for the feere thus hath she cried,
And weep, that it was pitee for to heere.
And ther-with-al Diane gan appeere,
With bowe in honde, right as an hunteresse,
And seide, 'Doghter, stint thin hevinesse.   1490
Among the goddes hie it is affermed,
And by eterne word writen and confermed,
Thou shalt ben wedded unto oon of tho
That han for thee so muchel care and wo;
But unto which of hem I may nat telle.
Farwel, for I ne may no lenger dwelle.
The fires which that on min auter brenne
Shul thee declare, er that thou go henne,
Thin aventure of love, as in this cas.'
And with that word, the arwes in the caas   1500
Of the goddesse clateren faste and ringe,
And forth she wente, and made a vanisshinge;
For which this Emelye astoned was,
And seide, 'What amounteth this, allas?
I putte me in thy proteccioun,

Diane, and in thy disposicioun.'
And hoom she goth anon the nexte weye.
This is th'effect, ther is namoore to seye.
  The nexte houre of Mars folwinge this,
Arcite unto the temple walked is   1510
Of fierse Mars, to doon his sacrifise,
With alle the rites of his paien wise.
With pitous herte and heigh devocioun,
Right thus to Mars he seide his orisoun:
'O stronge god, that in the regnes colde
Of Trace honoured art and lord yholde,
And hast in every regne and every lond
Of armes al the bridel in thin hond,
And hem fortunest as thee list devise,
Accepte of me my pitous sacrifise.   1520
If so be that my youthe may deserve,
And that my might be worthy for to serve
Thy godhede, that I may been oon of thine,
Than preye I thee to rewe upon my pine.
For thilke peine, and thilke hoote fir,
In which thow whilom brendest for desir,
Whan that thow usedest the beautee
Of faire, yonge, fresshe Venus free,
And haddest hir in armes at thy wille—
Although thee ones on a time misfille,   1530
Whan Vulcanus hadde caught thee in his las
And foond thee ligginge by his wife, allas.
For thilke sorwe that was in thin herte,
Have routhe as wel upon my peines smerte.
I am yong and unconninge, as thou woost,
And, as I trowe, with love offended moost,

That evere was any lives creature;
For she, that dooth me al this wo endure,
Ne reccheth nevere wher I sinke or fleete.
And wel I woot, er she me mercy heete,   1540
I moot with strengthe winne hir in the place;
And wel I woot, withouten help or grace
Of thee, ne may my strengthe noght availle.
Than help me, lord, tomorwe in my bataille,
For thilke fir that whilom brente thee
As wel as thilke fir now brenneth me;
And do that I tomorwe have victorye.
Min be the travaille, and thin be the glorye!
Thy soverein temple wol I moost honouren
Of any place, and alwey moost labouren   1550
In thy plesaunce and in thy craftes stronge,
And in thy temple I wol my baner honge,
And alle the armes of my compaignye;
And everemo, unto that day I die,
Eterne fir I wol biforn thee finde.
And eek to this avow I wol me binde:
My beerd, min heer that hongeth long adoun,
That nevere yet ne felte offensioun
Of rasour nor of shere, I wol the yeve,
And ben thy trewe servant whil I live.   1560
Now, lord, have routhe upon my sorwes soore,
Yif me the victorye, I aske thee namoore.'
    The preyere stint of Arcita the stronge,
The ringes on the temple-dore that honge,
And eek the dores, clatereden ful faste,
Of which Arcita somwhat him agaste.
The fires brenden upon the auter brighte,

That it gan al the temele for to lighte;
And sweete smel the ground anon upyaf,
And Arcita anon his hand uphaf,   1570
And moore encens into the fir he caste,
With othere rites mo; and atte laste
The statue of Mars bigan his hauberk ringe.
And with that soun he herde a murmuringe
Ful lowe and dim, that saide thus, 'Victorye.'
For which he yaf to Mars honour and glorye.
And thus with joye, and hope wel to fare,
Arcite anon unto his in is fare,
As fain as fowel is of the brighte sonne.
    And right anon swich strif ther is bigonne   1580
For thilke graunting, in the hevene above,
Bitwixe Venus, the goddesse of love,
And Mars, the sterne god armipotente,
That Jupiter was bisy it to stente;
Til that the pale Saturnus the colde,
That knew so manye of aventures olde,
Foond in his olde experience an art,
That he ful soone hath plesed every part.
As sooth is seid, elde hath greet avantage,
In elde is bothe wisdom and usage;   1590
Men may the olde at-renne, and noght at-rede.
Saturne anon, to stinten strif and drede,
Al be it that it is again his kinde,
Of al this strif he gan remedye finde.
'My deere doghter Venus,' quod Saturne,
'My cours, that hath so wide for to turne,
Hath moore power than woot any man.
Min is the drenching in the see so wan;

Min is the prison in the derke cote;
Min is the strangling and hanging by the throte; 1600
The murmure, and the cherles rebelling,
The groininge, and the privee empoisoning:
I do vengeance and plein correccioun,
Whil I dwelle in the signe of the leoun.
Min is the ruine of the hye halles,
The fallinge of the toures and of the walles
Upon the minour or the carpenter.
I slow Sampsoun shakinge the piler;
And mine be the maladies colde,
The derke tresons, and the castes olde; 1610
My looking is the fader of pestilence.
Now weep namoore, I shal doon diligence
That Palamon, that is thin owene knight,
Shal have his lady, as thou hast him hight.
Though Mars shal helpe his knight, yet nathelees
Bitwixe yow ther moot be som time pees,
Al be ye noght of o complexioun,
That causeth al day swich divisioun.
I am thin aiel, redy at thy wille;
Weep now namoore, I wol thy lust fulfille.' 1620
Now wol I stinten of the goddes above,
Of Mars, and of Venus, goddesse of love,
And telle yow, as pleinly as I can,
The grete effect, for which that I bigan.

Explicit tercia pars. Sequitur pars quarta.

Greet was the feeste in Atthenes that day,
And eek the lusty seson of that May
Made every wight to been in swich plesaunce,

That al that Monday justen they and daunce,
And spenden it in Venus heigh servise.
And by the cause that they sholde rise   1630
Eerly, for to seen the grete fight,
Unto hir reste wente they at night.
And on the morwe, whan that day gan springe,
Of hors and harneis noise and clateringe
Ther was in hostelries al aboute;
And to the paleis rood ther many a route
Of lordes, upon steedes and palfreys.
Ther maystow seen divisinge of harneis
So uncouth and so riche, and wroght so weel
Of goldsmithrye, of browdinge, and of steel;   1640
The sheeldes brighte, testeres, and trappures;
Gold-hewen helmes, hauberkes, cote-armures;
Lordes in parements on hir courseres,
Knightes of retenue, and eek squieres,
Nailinge the speres, and helmes bokelinge,
Gigginge of sheeldes, with layneres lacinge;
Thenede is, they weren nothing idel;
Themy steedes on the golden bridel
Gnawinge, and faste the armurers also
With file and hamer prikinge to and fro;   1650
Yemen on foote and communes many oon
With shorte staves, thicke as they may goon;
Pipes, trompes, nakers,[1] clariounes,
That in the bataille blowen blody sounes;
The paleis ful of peples up and doun,
Heere thre, ther ten, holdinge hir questioun,
Divininge of thise Thebane knightes two.

---

[1] *El*, nakerers.

Somme seiden thus, somme seide it shal be so;
Somme helden with him with the blake berd,   1659
Somme with the balled, somme with the thicke-herd;
Somme seide, he looked grim, and he wolde fighte;
'He hath a sparth of twenty pound of wighte.'
Thus was the halle ful of divininge,
Longe after that the sonne gan to springe.

　　The grete Theseus, that of his sleep awaked
With minstralcye and noise that was maked,
Held yet the chambre of his paleis riche,
Til that the Thebane knightes, bothe yliche
Honoured, were into the paleis fet.
Duk Theseus was at a window set,   1670
Arrayed right as he were a god in trone.
The peple preesseth thiderward ful soone
Him for to seen, and doon heigh reverence,
And eek to herkne his heste and his sentence.
An heraud on a scaffold made an 'Oo,'
Til al the noise of peple was ydo;
And whan he saugh the noise of peple al stille,
Tho shewed he the mighty dukes wille:
　　'The lord hath of his heigh discrecioun
Considered that it were destruccioun   1680
To gentil blood, to fighten in the gise
Of mortal bataille now in this emprise;
Wherfore, to shapen that they shal nat die,
He wol his firste purpos modifye.
No man therfor, up peine of los of lif,
No maner shot, polax, ne short knif
Into the listes sende, ne thider bringe;
Ne short swerd for to stoke, with point bitinge,

No man ne drawe, ne bere by his side.
Ne no man shal unto his felawe ride   1690
But o cours, with a sharp ygrounde spere;
Foine, if him list, on foote, himself to were;
And he that is at meschief shal be take,
And noght slain, but be broght unto the stake
That shal ben ordeined on either side;
But thider he shal by force and ther abide.
And if so falle, the chieftain be take
On outher side, or elles sleen his make,
No lenger shal the turneyinge laste.
God spede yow! Gooth forth, and ley on faste.   1700
With long swerd and with maces fighteth youre fille.
Gooth now youre wey; this is the lordes wille.'
   The vois of peple touched the hevene,
So loude cride they with murye stevene:
'God save swich a lord, that is so good,
He wilneth no destruccioun of blood!'
Up goon the trompes and the melodye.
And to the listes rit the compaignye
By ordinaunce, thurghout the citee large,
Hanged with clooth of gold, and nat with sarge.   1710
Ful lik a lord this noble duk gan ride,
Thise two Thebans upon either side;
And after rood the queene, and Emelye,
And after that another compaignye,
Of oon and oother, after hir degree.
And thus they passen thurghout the citee,
And to the listes come they by time.
It nas nat of the day yet fully prime,
Whan set was Theseus ful riche and hie,

Ypolita the quene, and Emelye,   1720
And other ladies in degrees aboute.
Unto the seetes preesseth al the route;
And westward, thurgh the gates under Marte,
Arcite, and eek the hondred of his parte,
With baner reed is entred right anon;
And in that selve moment Palamon
Is under Venus, estward in the place,
With baner whit, and hardy chiere and face.
In al the world, to seken up and doun,
So evene, withouten variacioun,   1730
Ther nere swiche compaignyes tweye.
For ther was noon so wis that coude seye,
That any hadde of oother avauntage
Of worthynesse, ne of estaat, ne age,
So evene were they[1] chosen, for to gesse.
And in two renges faire they hem dresse.
Whan that hir names rad were everichon,
That in hir nombre gile were ther noon,
Tho were the gates shet, and cried was loude:
'Do now youre devoir, yonge knightes proude!' 1740
   The heraudes lefte hir priking up and doun;
Now ringen trompes loude, and clarioun;
Ther is namoore to seyn, but west and est
In goon the speres ful sadly in arrest;
In gooth the sharpe spore into the side.
Ther seen men who can juste, and who can ride;
Ther shiveren shaftes upon sheeldes thicke;
He feeleth thurgh the herte-spoon the pricke.
Up springen speres twenty foot on highte;

    [1] *El, om*, they.

Out gooth the swerdes as the silver brighte.   1750
The helmes they tohewen and toshrede;
Out brest the blood, with stierne stremes rede.
With mighty maces the bones they tobreste.
He thurgh the thickeste of the throng gan threste.
Ther stomblen[1] steedes stronge, and doun gooth alle.
He rolleth under foot as dooth a balle;
He foineth on his feet with his tronchoun,
And he him hurtleth with his hors adoun.
He thurgh the body is hurt, and sithen ytake,
Maugree his heed, and broght unto the stake,   1760
As forward was, right there he moste abide;
Another lad is on that oother side.
And som time dooth hem Theseus to reste,
Hem to fresshen, and drinken if hem leste.
Ful ofte aday han thise Thebanes two
Togidre ymet, and wroght his felawe wo;
Unhorsed hath ech oother of hem tweye.
Ther nas no tigre in the vale of Galgopheye,
Whan that hir whelpe is stole, whan it is lite,
So crueel on the hunte, as is Arcite   1770
For jelous herte upon this Palamoun;
Ne in Belmarye ther nis so fel leoun,
That hunted is, or for his hunger wood,
Ne of his praye desireth so the blood,
As Palamon to sleen his foo Arcite.
The jelous strokes on hir helmes bite;
Out renneth blood on bothe hir sides rede.
    Som time an ende ther is of every dede;
For er the sonne unto the reste wente,

[1] *El*, semblen.

The stronge king Emetreus gan hente 1780
This Palamon, as he faught with Arcite,
And made his swerd depe in his flessh to bite;
And by the force of twenty is he take
Unyolden, and ydrawen unto the stake.
And in the rescus of this Palamoun
The stronge king Lygurge is born adoun;
And king Emetreus, for al his strengthe,
Is born out of his sadel a swerdes lengthe—
So hitte him Palamon er he were take;
But al for noght, he was broght to the stake. 1790
His hardy herte mighte him helpe naught;
He moste abide, whan that he was caught,
By force, and eek by composicioun.

    Who sorweth now but woful Palamoun,
That moot namoore goon again to fighte?
And whan that Theseus hadde seyn this sighte,
Unto the folk that foghten thus echon
He cride, 'Hoo! namoore, for it is doon!
I wol be trewe juge, and no partye.
Arcite of Thebes shal have Emelye, 1800
That by his fortune hath hir faire ywonne.'
Anon ther is a noise of peple bigonne
For joye of this, so loude and heighe withalle,
It semed that the listes sholde falle.

    What can now faire Venus doon above?
What seith she now? What dooth this queene of love
But wepeth so, for wantinge of hir wille,
Til that hir teeres in the listes fille?
She seide, 'I am ashamed, doutelees.'
Saturnus seide, 'Doghter, hoold thy pees. 1810

Mars hath his wille, his knight hath al his boone,
And, by min heed, thou shalt been esed soone.'
    The trompes with the loude minstralcye,
The heraudes, that ful loude yolle and crye,
Been in hir wele for joye of daun Arcite.
But herkneth me, and stinteth now a lite,
Which a miracle ther bifel anon.
This fierse Arcite hath of his helm ydon,
And on a courser, for to shewe his face,
He priketh endelong the large place,   1820
Lokinge upward upon this¹ Emelye;
And she again him caste a freendlich eye,
[For wommen, as to speken in comune,
They folwen al the favour of fortune,]²
And³ was al his chiere, as in his herte.
Out of the ground a furye infernal sterte,
From Pluto sent, at requeste of Saturne,
For which his hors for fere gan to turne,
And leepe aside, and foundred as he leepe;
And, er that Arcite may taken keepe,   1830
He pighte him on the pomel of his heed,
That in the place he lay as he were deed,
His brest tobrosten with his sadel-bowe.
As blak he lay as any cole or crowe,
So was the blood yronnen in his face.
Anon he was yborn out of the place,
With herte soor, to Theseus paleis.
Tho was he corven out of his harneis,
And in a bed ybrought ful faire and blive,

¹ *El, om.* this.   ² ll 1823–34 do not occur in *El,* **Hg,** or *Gg.*
³ *Hg,* And she.

For he was yet in memorye and alive, 1840
And alwey cryinge after Emelye.
　　Duk Theseus, with al his compaignye,
Is comen hoom to Atthenes his citee,
With alle blisse and greet solempnitee.
Al be it that this aventure was falle,
He nolde noght disconforten hem alle.
Men seide eek, that Arcite shal nat die,
He shal been heled of his maladye.
And of another thing they weren as fain,
That of hem alle was ther noon yslain, 1850
Al were they soore yhurt, and namely oon,
That with a spere was thirled his brest-boon.
To othere woundes, and to broken armes,
Somme hadden salves, and somme hadden charmes,
Fermacies of herbes, and eek save
They dronken, for they wolde hir limes[1] have.
For which this noble duk, as he wel can,
Conforteth and honoureth every man,
And made revel al the longe night,
Unto the straunge lordes, as was right. 1860
Ne ther was holden no disconfitinge,
But as a justes or a tourneyinge;
For soothly ther was no disconfiture,
For falling nis nat but an aventure;
Ne to be lad by force unto the stake
Unyolden, and with twenty knightes take,
O persone allone, withouten mo,
And haried forth by arm, foot, and too,
And eke his steede driven forth with staves,

[1] *Cp*, lives.

With footmen, bothe yemen and eek knaves— 1870
It nas aretted him no vileinye;
Ther may no man clepen it cowardye.
  For which anon duk Theseus leet crye,
To stinten alle rancour and envye,
The gree as wel of a side as of oother,
And either side ylik, as ootheres brother;
And yaf hem yiftes after hir degree,
And fully heeld a feeste dayes three,
And convoyed the kinges worthily
Out of his toun a journee largely. 1880
And hoom wente every man the right way.
Ther was namoore, but 'fare wel, have good day!'
Of this bataille I wol namoore endite,
But speke of Palamon and of Arcite.
  Swelleth the brest of Arcite, and the soore
Encreesseth at his herte moore and moore.
The clothered blood, for any lechecraft,
Corrupteth, and is in his bouk ylaft,
That neither veine blood, ne ventusinge,
Ne drinke of herbes may ben his helpinge. 1890
The vertu expulsif, or animal,
Fro thilke vertu cleped natural
Ne may the venim voiden, ne expelle.
The pipes of his longes gonne to swelle,
And every lacerte in his brest adoun
Is shent with venim and corrupcioun.
Him gaineth neither, for to gete his lif,
Vomit upward, ne dounward laxatif;
Al is tobrosten thilke regioun.
Nature hath now no dominacioun; 1900

And certeinly, ther Nature wol nat wirche,
Farewel, physik! Go ber the man to chirche.
This al and som, that Arcita moot die,
For which he sendeth after Emelye,
And Palamon, that was his cosin deere.
Than seide he thus, as ye shul after heere:
  'Naught may the woful spirit in min herte
Declare o point of alle my sorwes smerte
To yow, my lady, that I love moost;
But I biquethe the service of my goost   1910
To yow aboven every creature,
Sin that my lif may no lenger dure.
Allas, the wo! allas, the peines stronge,
That I for yow have suffred, and so longe!
Allas, the deeth! allas, min Emelye!
Allas, departing of oure compaignye!
Allas, min hertes queene! allas, my wif!
Min hertes lady, endere of my lif!
What is this world? What asketh men to have?
Now with his love, now in his colde grave   1920
Allone, withouten any compaignye.
Farewel, my sweete foo! min Emelye!
And softe taak me in youre armes tweye,
For love of God, and herkneth what I seye.
  I have heer with my cosin Palamon
Had strif and rancour, many a day agon,
For love of yow, and for my jalousye.
And Juppiter so wis my soule gye,
To speken of a servaunt proprely,
With alle circumstaunces trewely—   1930
That is to seyn, trouthe, honour, knighthede,

Wisdom, humblesse, estaat, and heigh kinrede,
Fredom, and al that longeth to that art—
So Juppiter have of my soule part,
As in this world right now ne knowe I non
So worthy to be loved as Palamon,
That serveth yow, and wol doon al his lif.
And if that evere ye shul been a wif,
Foryet nat Palamon, the gentil man.'
And with that word his speche faille gan,   1940
For from his feet[1] up to his brest was come
The coold of deeth, that hadde him overcome.
And yet moore over: for in hise armes two
The vital strengthe is lost, and al ago.
Oonly the intellect, withouten moore,
That dwelled in his herte sik and sore,
Gan faillen, whan the herte felte deeth.
Dusked his eyen two, and failled breeth,
But on his lady yet caste he his eye;
His laste word was, 'Mercy, Emelye!'   1950
His spirit chaunged hous, and wente ther
As I cam nevere, I can nat tellen wher.
Therfor I stinte, I nam no divinistre;
Of soules finde I nat in this registre,
Ne me ne list thilke opiniouns to telle
Of hem, though that they writen wher they dwelle.
Arcite is coold, ther Mars his soule gye;
Now wol I speken forth of Emelye.
   Shrighte Emelye, and howleth Palamon,
And Theseus his suster took anon   1960
Swowninge, and baar hir fro the corps away.

              [1] *Hg. Cp*; *El,* And from his herte.

What helpeth it to tarien forth the day,
To tellen how she weepe, both eve and morwe?
For in swich cas wommen have swich sorwe,
Whan that hir housbond is from hem ago,
That for the moore part they sorwen so,
Or ellis fallen in swich maladye,
That at the laste certeinly they die.

    Infinite been the sorwes and the teeres
Of olde folk, and folk of tendre yeres,   1970
In al the toun, for deeth of this Theban,
For him ther wepeth bothe child and man;
So greet a weping was ther noon, certain,
Whan Ector was ybroght, al fressh yslain,
To Troye. Allas! the pitee that was ther,
Cracchinge of chekes, rentinge eek of heer.
'Why woldestow be deed,' thise wommen crye,
'And haddest gold ynough, and Emelye?'
No man mighte gladen Theseus,
Savinge his olde fader Egeus,   1980
That knew this worldes transmutacioun,
As he hadde seyn it[1] up and doun,
Joye after wo, and wo after gladnesse;
And shewed hem ensamples and liknesse:

    'Right as ther died nevere man,' quod he,
'That he ne livede in erthe in som degree,
Right so ther livede nevere man,' he seide,
'In al this world, that som time he ne deide.
This world nis but a thurghfare ful of wo,
And we been pilgrimes, passinge to and fro;   1990
Deeth is an ende of every worldes soore.'

            [1] *Hg*, it chaungen bothe up.

And over al this yet seide he muchel moore
To this effect, ful wisely to enhorte
The peple, that they sholde hem reconforte.
   Duk Theseus, with al his bisy cure,
Caste[1] now wher that the sepulture
Of goode Arcite may best ymaked be,
And eek moost honurable in his degree.
And at the laste he took conclusioun
That, ther as first Arcite and Palamoun   2000
Hadden for love the bataille hem bitwene,
That in that selve grove, swoote and grene,
Ther as he hadde his amorouse desires,
His compleinte, and for love hise hoote fires,
He wolde make a fir, in which the office
Funeral he mighte al accomplice;
And leet comande anon to hacke and hewe
The okes olde, and leye hem on a rewe
In colpons wel arrayed for to brenne;
Hise officers with swifte feet they renne,   2010
And ride anon at his comandement.
And after this, Theseus hath ysent
After a beere, and it al overspradde
With clooth of gold, the richeste that he hadde.
And of the same suite he cladde Arcite;
Upon hise hondes hadde he gloves white;
Eek on his heed a coroune of laurer grene,
And in his hond a swerd ful bright and kene.
He leide him, bare the visage, on the beere,
Therwith he weepe, that pitee was to heere.   2020
And for the peple sholde seen him alle,

---

[1] *Hg*; *E*, *Gg*, *Cp*, Cast.

Whan it was day, he broghte him to the halle,
That roreth of the crying and the soun.
   Tho cam this woful Theban Palamoun,
With flotery berd, and rugged asshy heeres,
In clothes blake, ydropped al with teeres;
And, passinge othere of wepinge, Emelye,
The rewefulleste of al the compaignye.
In as muche as the service sholde be
The moore noble and riche in his degree,   2030
Duk Theseus leet forth thre steedes bringe,
That trapped were in steel al gliteringe,
And covered with the armes of daun Arcite.
Upon thise steedes, grete and white,
Ther sitten folk, of which oon baar his sheeld,
Another his spere in his hondes heeld;
The thridde baar with him his bowe Turkeis,
Of brend gold was the caas, and eek the harneis;
And riden forth a paas with sorweful cheere
Toward the grove, as ye shul after heere.   2040
The nobleste of the Grekes that ther were
Upon hir shuldres carieden the bere,
With slak paas, and eyen rede and wete,
Thurghout the citee, by the maister strete,
That sprad was al with blak, and wonder hye
Right of the same is the strete ywrye.
Upon the right hond wente old Egeus,
And on that oother side Duk Theseus,
With vessel in hir hand of gold ful fin,
Al ful of hony, milk, and blood, and win;   2050
Eek Palamon, with ful greet compaignye;
And after that cam woful Emelye,

With fir in honde, as was that time the gise,
To do the office of funeral servise.

Heigh labour, and ful greet apparaillinge
Was at the service and the fir-makinge,
That with his grene tope the hevene raughte,
And twenty fadme of brede the armes straughte;
This is to seyn, the bowes were so brode.
Of stree first ther was leid ful many a lode.   2060
But how the fir was maked up on highte,
Ne eek the names that the trees highte,
As ook, firre, birch, asp, alder, holm, popeler,
Wilugh, elm, plane, assh, box, chastein, linde, laurer,
Mapul, thorn, bech, hasel, ew, whippeltree,
How they weren feld[1], shal nat be toold for me;
Ne hou the goddes ronnen up and doun,
Disherited of hir habitacioun,
In which they woneden in reste and pees,
Nymphes[2], Fawnes, and Amadrides;   2070
Ne hou the beestes and the briddes alle
Fledden for fere, whan the wode was falle;
Ne how the ground agast was of the light,
That was nat wont to seen the sonne bright;
Ne how the fir was couched first with stree,
And thanne with drye stockes, cloven a thre,
And thanne with grene wode and spicerye,
And thanne with clooth of gold and with perrye,
And gerlandes hanginge with ful many a flour,
The mirre, th'encens, with al so greet odour;   2080
Ne how Arcite lay among al this,
Ne what richesse aboute his body is;

[1] *El*, fild.   [2] *Hg, Cp*; *El, Gg*, Nymphus.

Ne how that Emelye, as was the gise,
Putte in the fir of funeral servise;
Ne how she swowned whan men made fir,
Ne what she spak, ne what was hir desir;
Ne what jeweles men in the fire caste,
Whan that the fir was greet and brente faste;
Ne how somme caste hir sheeld, and somme hir spere,
And of hir vestiments, whiche that they were,   2090
And coppes fulle of win, and milk, and blood,
Into the fir, that brente as it were wood;
Ne how the Grekes with an huge route
Thries [1] riden al the place aboute
Upon the left hand, with a loud shoutinge,
And thries with hir speres clateringe;
And thries how the ladies gonne crye;
And how that lad was homward Emelye;
Ne how Arcite is brent to asshen colde;
Ne how that lich-wake was yholde   2100
Al thilke night, ne how the Grekes pleye
The wake-pleyes, ne kepe I nat to seye;
Who wrastleth best naked, with oille enoint,
Ne who that baar him best, in no disjoint.
I wol nat tellen eek how that they goon
Hoom til Atthenes whan the pley is doon.
But shortly to the point than wol I wende,
And maken of my longe tale an ende.
    By processe and by lengthe of certein yeres
Al stinted is the moorninge and the teres   2110
Of Grekes, by oon general assent.
Than semed me ther was a parlement

[1] *El*, Tries.

At Atthenes, upon certein points and caas;
Among the whiche points yspoken was
To have with certein contrees alliaunce,
And have fully of Thebans obeisaunce.
For which this noble Theseus anon
Leet senden after gentil Palamon,
Unwist of him what was the cause and why;
But in hise blake clothes sorwefully   2120
He cam at his comandement in hye.
Tho sente Theseus for Emelye.
Whan they were set, and hust was al the place,
And Theseus abiden hadde a space,
Er any word cam from his wise brest,
His eyen sette he ther as was his lest,
And with a sad visage he siked stille,
And after that right thus he seide his wille:
  'This firste moevere of the cause above,
Whan he first made the faire cheine of love,   2130
Greet was th'effect, and heigh was his entente;
Wel wiste he why, and what therof he mente;
For with that faire cheine of love he bond
The fir, the eir, the water, and the lond
In certein boundes, that they may nat flee;
That same prince and that same moevere,' quod he,
'Hath stablissed, in this wrecched world adoun,
Certeine dayes and duracioun
To al that is engendred in this place,
Over the whiche day they may nat pace,   2140
Al mowe they yet tho dayes wel abregge;
Ther nedeth noght noon auctoritee allegge,[1]

      [1] *Hg*, to allegge.

For it is preeved by experience,
But that me list declaren my sentence.
Than may men by this ordre wel discerne
That thilke moevere stable is and eterne.
Wel may men knowe, but it be a fool,
That every part dirriveth from his hool.
For nature hath taken his biginning
Of no partye or of cantel of a thing,   2150
But of a thing that parfit is and stable,
Descendinge so, til it be corrumpable.
And therfore, of his wise purveyaunce,
He hath so wel biset his ordinaunce,
That speces of thinges and progressiouns
Shullen enduren by successiouns,
And nat eterne be, withoute lie:
This maystow understonde and seen at[1] eye.

    Loo, the ook, that hath so long a norisshinge
From time that it first biginneth springe,   2160
And hath so long a lif, as we may see,
Yet at the laste wasted is the tree.

    Considereth eek, how that the harde stoon
Under oure feet, on which we trede and goon,
Yet wasteth it, as it lith by the weye.
The brode river somtime wexeth dreye.
The grete tounes[2] se we wane and wende.
Thanne may ye se that al this thing hath ende.

    Of man and womman seen we wel also,
That nedeth in oon of thise termes two,   2170
This is to seyn, in youthe or elles age,
He moot be deed, the king as shal a page;

---

[1] *El*, it.   [2] *El*, toures.

Som in his bed, som in the depe see,
Som in the large feeld, as men may see.
Ther helpeth noght, al goth that ilke weye.
Thanne may I seyn that[1] al this thing moot deye.
What maketh this but Juppiter the king
That is prince and cause of alle thing,
Convertinge al unto his propre welle,
From which it is dirrived, sooth to tell?   2180
And heer-agains no creature on live
Of no degree availleth for to strive.

   Thanne is it wisdom, as it thinketh me,
To maken vertu of necessitee,
And take it weel, that we may nat eschue,
And namely that to us alle is due.
And whoso gruccheth ought, he dooth folye,
And rebel is to him that al may gye.
And certeinly a man hath moost honour
To dien in his excellence and flour,   2190
Whan he is siker of his goode name;
Than hath he doon his freend, ne him, no shame.
And gladder oghte his freend been of his deeth,
Whan with honour upyolden is his breeth,
Than whan his name apalled is for age;
For al forgeten is his vassellage.
Thanne is it best, as for a worthy fame,
To dien whan that he is best of name.
The contrarye of al this is wilfulnesse.
Why grucchen we? Why have we hevinesse,   2200
That goode Arcite, of chivalrye flour,
Departed is, with duetee and honour,

---

[1] *El, om.* that.

Out of this foule prisoun of this lif?
Why grucchen heere his cosin and his wif
Of his welfare that loved hem so weel?
Can he hem thank? Nay, God woot, never a deel,
That bothe his soule and eek hemself offende,
And yet they mowe hir lustes nat amende.
 What may I concluden of this longe serie,
But after wo I rede us to be merye,   2210
And thanken Juppiter of al his grace?
And er that we departen from this place,
I rede we make, of sorwes two,
O parfit joye, lastinge everemo:
And loketh now, wher moost sorwe is herinne,
Ther wol we first amenden and biginne.'
 'Suster,' quod he, 'this is my fulle assent,
With al th'avis heere of my parlement,
That gentil Palamon, thin owene knight,
That serveth yow with wille, herte, and might, 2220
And evere hath doon, sin that ye first him knewe,
That ye shul, of youre grace, upon him rewe,
And taken him for housbonde and for lord:
Lene me youre hond, for this is oure accord.
Lat se now of youre wommanly pitee.
He is a kinges brother sone, pardee;
And, though he were a poure bacheler,
Sin he hath served yow so many a yeer,
And had for yow so greet adversitee,
It moste been considered, leeveth me; 2230
For gentil mercy oghte to passen right.'
 Than seide he thus to Palamon ful right:
'I trowe ther nedeth litel sermoning

To make yow assente to this thing.
Com neer, and taak youre lady by the hond.'
Bitwixen hem was maad anon the bond
That highte matrimoigne or mariage,
By al the conseil and the baronage.
And thus with alle blisse and melodye
Hath Palamon ywedded Emelye.   2240
And God, that al this wide world hath wroght,
Sende him his love, that hath[1] it deere aboght.
For now is Palamon in alle wele,
Livinge in blisse, in richesse, and in heele;
And Emelye him loveth so tendrely,
And he hir serveth so gentilly,
That nevere was ther no word hem bitwene
Of jalousye, or any oother teene.
    Thus endeth 'Palamon and Emelye';
And God save all this faire compaignye! Amen. 2250

[1] *El, om.* hath.

Heere is ended the knightes tale.

NOTES

1. In several MSS. the following quotation from a passage in
   Statius's *Thebaid*, describing the return of Theseus to Athens,
   occurs in the margin or at the head of this tale:

   > Iamque domos patrias, Scithice post aspera gentis
   > Prelia, laurigero, etc.   (*Theb*. XII, 519.)

   (And now [Theseus approaching] his native land in his
   laurelled [car] after his fierce battles with the Scythians [is
   received with glad applause.])

   These lines, added by copyists, give us a hint of the 'olde
   stories' that Chaucer had in mind. The *Thebaid* is an epic
   poem about the war of the seven heroes against Thebes,
   published about A.D. 91. The tradition that Statius was con-
   verted to Christianity was partly responsible for its popularity
   in medieval times. Chaucer gives a long summary of it in
   Troilus and Criseyde (V, 1485 ff.); and Criseyde herself is
   found reading the 'romaunce of Thebes' (II, 100–108).
   Boccaccio drew on it for certain details of the *Teseida*.

   Theseus, after his desertion of Ariadne (a subject treated by
   Chaucer in his *Legend of Good Women*) had become King of
   Athens and set out on an expedition against the Amazons, a
   race of warrior-women living in the kingdom called by
   Boccaccio *Scizia* (Scythia), but by Chaucer—and his friend the
   poet Gower—*Femenye* (from *femina*). Theseus, according to
   legend, carried off Antiope, sister of the Amazonian Queen
   Hippolyta. Statius altered this story by substituting Hippo-
   lyta for Antiope, and Boccaccio and Chaucer followed him.
   In describing the Theseus of legend as a 'duke of Athens'
   Chaucer is following Boccaccio; but he doubtless knew that
   the title was in use in his own day, being held by a Constable
   of France who was killed at the battle of Poitiers.

   Shakespeare, who had evidently read the Knight's Tale, like-
   wise calls Theseus 'Duke of Athens' in *A Midsummer Night's*

Dream,[1] as does Fletcher in *The Two Noble Kinsmen*, a play which owes its plot and some of its details to the Tale.

17–27. A notable example of *occupatio*, the rhetorical device by which a writer lists briefly the themes that he does not intend to treat in full (*cf.* Hebrews xi, 32 ff.); the events that Chaucer summarizes in ll. 6–27 take up over one hundred and forty stanzas in Boccaccio's *Teseida*.

Chaucer uses *occupatio* again in ll. 136, 1339–48, and elsewhere. In contrast to the French and Italian writers of romances, he rarely indulges in epic fullness and digressions; 'to th'effect' is his motto.

26. Neither Statius nor Boccaccio speaks of any 'tempest'; indeed, Boccaccio says the journey was made without difficulty. There are three possibilities:

1. That Chaucer has in mind the phrase "con (sí) gran tempesta" (*Tes.* II, 55), which Boccaccio uses to describe the force of Theseus's later attack on Creon. Chaucer disposes of this assault in four lines (128–132) as against Boccaccio's one hundred and sixty.

2. 'Tempest' was occasionally used in the fourteenth century to mean 'commotion,' and may therefore conceivably represent 'tomolto,' the word Boccaccio uses to describe the crowds that throng to welcome Theseus on his arrival (*Tes.* II, 24; *cf.* *K.T.* 47–48).

3. That it is an oblique reference to the storm that occurred when Anne of Bohemia landed in England for her marriage with Richard II in 1382. But there seems no good reason why the Knight should refer to this.

55–56. The swoon is Chaucer's addition. He dwells on the poignancy of similar situations in other tales (*e.g.*, the *Canterbury Tales*, B 645–654, 854 ff.). Like Dante, he believed that pity for women and children in distress "renneth sone in gentil herte" (*cf.* 903 and note); thus l. 56 is in accord with

---

[1] But this title was also used in an earlier play; see N. Coghill, 'Shakespeare's reading in Chaucer,' in *Elizabethan and Jacobean Studies presented to F. P. Wilson* (Oxford 1959).

the character of the "parfit gentil knight" who is telling the story.

67. Fortune is often represented in medieval art (*e.g.*, in the fine but partly destroyed painting on the north wall of the choir of Rochester Cathedral, which Chaucer probably saw) as a Queen controlling an ever-moving wheel that swings people to temporal prosperity or to disaster. Boethius (*d.* 524), whose *De Consolatione Philosophiæ* Chaucer translated (see p. 20), took the view that these mutations are themselves subject to a higher power (Book 1, Prose 6), and this is elaborated by Dante (*Inferno* VII, 78 ff.). Chaucer's concern with Fortune is constant throughout his poetry, and he devoted a series of Balades to the theme. In the present lines the reference to Fortune ('who keeps no state of affairs stable in happiness'; 68) is developed from an allusion in the *Teseida* made by Teseo when replying to the mourners later. The similar references in 228, 394, are also added by Chaucer.

For the temple of *Clemency* see p. 27.

73. *wepe and waille*. A favourite phrase of Chaucer's, which has no equivalent in Boccaccio. Chaucer's frequent use of such popular alliterative combinations helps to give an easy colloquial quality to his verse (*cf.* 358).

74. Cappaneus, one of the seven heroes who took part in the siege of Thebes, was married to Evadne. Zeus struck him by lightning for boasting. In Chaucer's *Troilus and Criseyde* Cassandra tells Troilus

how Cappaneus the proude
With thondir-dint was slaine, that cride aloude. (V, 1504.)

84. "To do shameful wrong to the corpses of all our lords." The mention of *vileinye*, like the description of the duke as *gentil* (94), is another knightly touch.

94. In Statius and Boccaccio, and in Chaucer's *Anelida and Arcite* (see p. 17), Theseus is riding in a chariot.

108. The 'displaying' of the banner is the signal for war.

110. *Go ne ride*. One of several emphatic traditional antitheses; cf. *looth or lief*, 979. 'Go' = 'walk,' and the sense of the phrase is 'go by any means, on any account.'

117–118 Chaucer has inserted this detail. Mars ('ruddy of colour' because his planet is red) is the proper emblem for a war-banner, but is specially appropriate for the war-like and impetuous Theseus, who swears by him in l. 850 (another insertion by Chaucer), as well as in the *Legend of Good Women* (2109).

119. Cf. *Anelida and Arcite* (40–41), where it is said that when Hippolyta entered Athens,

> Al the ground about her char she spradde
> With brightnesse of the beaute in her face.

There is an even closer parallel in the *Bruce*, a poem by the fourteenth-century Scottish poet Barbour:

> Their speris, their pennownis and their scheldis
> Of licht illuminit all the feldis. (VIII, 227–228.)

Similar expressions are to be found in Old French. There is thus no need to resort to Skeat's forced explanation of *feeldes* as referring to the surfaces on which charges are displayed; *feeldes* is not evidenced in this heraldic sense before 1400, and the plural form would be odd in this sense at any time.

120. The pennon 'enriched with gold' is another addition by Chaucer. It was part of a knight's equipment, carried on the top of his spear, and usually, as here, bearing his cognizance.

Pennons are often described as *ybete* ('beaten'), but it is not always clear whether the meaning is 'stamped, branded,' or 'embroidered'; the records of St Mary at Hill for the year 1426 speak of the "beting and steininge" of "bokeram [buckram] pinouns."

Chaucer had told the story of Theseus's encounter with the Minotaur of Crete in the *Legend of Good Women* (1928).

129–130. *manly as a knight in plein bataille*, i.e., in single combat in the course of a pitched battle. Like most phrases relating to the art of war, "in plein bataille" is of French origin. Chaucer, like his own knight, had served in the tented field, and knew far more of war and chivalry than Boccaccio did; there is no equivalent phrase in the *Teseida*.

158 ff. Boccaccio speaks only of their armour, not of their coat-of-arms; the heraldic devices indicating their family would be recognized by heralds, whose function it was to identify knights by such bearings (which would show them as ransomable: *cf.* l. 166). These lines further show Chaucer's familiarity with fourteenth-century warfare.

171. *Terme of his lif.* Originally a legal phrase, but found in at least one other romance.

174. *for everemoore.* A rhetorical exaggeration.

176. The references to May and its observances—so appropriate to the spring morning on which the tale is supposedly being told—have been added by Chaucer. The observances are usually associated with the first of May (cf. *Legend of Good Women*, F 108), on which day may-garlands (*cf.* 196) are still to be seen in some English towns. In illustrations of 'the occupations of the months' — a favourite subject of medieval art—May is sometimes represented by a maiden with a garland.

178–180. The description, perfectly suited to the tone of the tale, was perhaps *suggested* by Boccaccio's account of Emilia's plucking 'with her white hand the fresh-blown rose.'

197. *hevenisshly.* A favourite adverb of Chaucer's. Boccaccio describes her as singing love-songs 'with angelic voice and glad heart.'

217. "closely barred with many large square bars of iron."

219. By making Palamon the first to see Emily Chaucer alters the disposition of Boccaccio's story (*cf.* p. 28) so that the lover who is the first to see her is the one who eventually weds her.

A similar situation is described in *The Kingis Quair* of James I, King of Scotland (1394–1437); though James was doubtless influenced by the Knight's Tale, some of the circumstances may well have been duplicated in his own life: he spent some eighteen years in an English prison, and married the heroine of the poem. And in Stendhal's *Chartreuse de Parme*, set in nineteenth-century Italy, the hero, imprisoned in a tower, falls in love with the governor's daughter whom he glimpses from his window.

229. The position ('aspect') of the planets in regard to one another and jointly in regard to the earth was thought to have great influence on human actions; and their position at the time of a man's birth—their 'constellation'—was especially important (see *Prologue*, 413–414, and Appendix III). The belief that the planets in their turn are subject to a higher power is glanced at in l. 251.

That Fortune and the planets were not necessarily thought of as identical is confirmed by Gower's *Confessio Amantis* (written *c.* 1390):

> ... som men write
> And sein that fortune is to wite,
> And som men hold opinioun
> That it is constellacioun
> Which causeth all that a man doth.
>
> (*Prologue*, 529 ff.)

The aspect of Saturn is generally malignant. (*Cf.* 1595 ff.)

231. *although we hadde it sworn* = 'although we had sworn to the contrary, despite all we can do.' Skeat quotes a close parallel from the romance of *Sir Perceval*:

> Thofe the rede knight had sworne,
> Out of his sadille is he borne. (61–62.)

235–236. Literally, 'thou hast a fantastic idea in regard to this belief': *i.e.* 'this belief [that you have just expressed] has been prompted by a false conception [of what has happened].'

238–239. Chaucer has added this image, one common in the literature of courtly love. In the *Roman de la Rose* the lover tells how Cupid

> Shette at me so wonder smerte
> That through min eye unto min herte
> The takel smot, and depe it wente.
>
> (Chaucer's translation, 1728–30.)

246 ff. This prayer (Chaucer's invention) may be compared with Palamon's longer prayer to Venus in 1263 ff.

274. Oaths of brotherhood between friends or relatives were regarded in the Middle Ages as more sacred than ties of blood. In the romance of *Amis and Amiloun* Amis is prepared to sacrifice his own children to keep his pledge to his friend Amiloun.

275. "even though we had to suffer death by torture," Old French 'mourir en la peine.'

276. "till death us depart [=divide]" was the original phrasing of the words in the Marriage Service that now run "till death us do part."

277. *to hindre* represents a change of construction, likely enough in speech delivered under emotional stress (*cf.* the changes in tense at 279–280, 291–292).

295–301. "It is more likely that you are false than that I am . . . for it is I who first loved her with passionate love [as a lover loves his mistress] . . . yours is a feeling of religious devoutness, mine is one of human love."

304 ff. This series of arguments is introduced by Chaucer, who was continually pondering the nature, value, and effects of love. The 'old writer' (305) is Boethius: in his *De Consolatione Philosophiæ*, Book III, Metre 12, Philosophy sings the tale of Eurydice and Orpheus, who is 'given a law' that he shall not look back till he is out of hell. But "Quis legem det amantibus? maior lex amor est sibi." 306 ff. closely resemble Chaucer's rendering of this line in his prose translation of Boethius, which runs: "But what is he that may yive a lawe to loveres? Love is a gretter lawe and a strenger to himself than any lawe that man may yeven." (This last clause supports the Ellesmere reading *of* in l. 308, as against the other MSS.)

For the ethical aspect of the situation we may compare Sir Thomas Malory's account of the rivalry between Sir Tristram and Sir Palomides for La Beall Isode: when Tristram accuses Palomides of 'treason,' he replies, "Sir, I have done to you no treson, for love is fre for all men, and thoughe I have loved your lady, she is my lady as well as youres." (*Works of Sir Thomas Malory*, ed. E. Vinaver, II, 781.)

309. *positif lawe*, formal, enacted law, as distinct from the law of nature.

311. *maugree his heed*. An adaptation of the French 'maugré sa teste,' 'despite all he can do.' Medieval English had a variety of such expressions (*cf.* l. 938).

314-315. "Moreover, it is unlikely that you will ever [have an opportunity to] win her favour."

319. The reference is apparently to Æsop's fable of "The Lion, the Tiger [or Bear], and the Fox."

323. "At the king's court every man for himself," evidently a proverbial expression.

329. Chaucer completely omits Boccaccio's account of Emilia's discovery of the two prisoners and her subsequent behaviour (see p. 28). On the other hand, in Boccaccio there is as yet ho hint of their bitter jealousy, his equivalent to l. 329 being:

> Grandi erano *i sospiri* e *il tormento*
> De ciascheduno.   (*Tes. III*, 46).
> ('Great were the sighs and torment of each.')

340-343. This slight digression (or '*diversio*,' as the rhetoricians would call it) is Chaucer's. But in classical story Theseus did not go to hell to rescue Pirithous; he accompanied him on his journey thither to carry off Proserpina. *Cf.* Ovid's *Epistolæ ex Ponto*:

> Pirithoun Theseus Stygias comitavit ad undas. (III, iii, 43.)

Chaucer is following the *Roman de la Rose*, which in ll. 8148–54 misinterprets Ovid's other reference to the story:

> Thesea Pirithous non tam sensisset amicum
> Si non infernas vivus adisset aquas.
>   (*Tristia* I, v, 19–20.)

(Pirithous would not have felt the strength of Theseus's friendship so much, if he had not gone, while still alive, to the waters below.)

3. Chaucer momentarily disregards the circumstance that the tale is being narrated by the knight to his fellow-pilgrims, though at l. 350 he himself reminds us of this.

354. *o stounde*, "for a single moment," "at any time." Only one MS. (Camb. Dd. 4. 24) reads *o*, the rest having *or*, or variants including *or* (probably because it follows *or night*).

359. The omission of the pronoun and change of tense (though one MS. has *took*) are not uncommon in medieval English, which is often closer to loose colloquial usage than modern 'literary' English.

364. "He watches for a chance of committing suicide secretly."

365–416. This lament, broadening out into philosophical speculation, is Chaucer's invention.

367. "Now it is decreed for me," *i.e.*, 'now I am destined.'

373–374. Arcite's references to Emily are always in terms of *grace* and *mercy*; and it is enough if he but see her: *cf.* ll. 262–263, 315, 373–374, 381, 387, 391 (*wanhope*—despair of the mercy of God—being one of the other theological terms borrowed from Christianity by the religion of love), and 415. This lends irony to the later description of his victory: for it is just when he is gazing on her "and she again him caste a freendlich eye" (1821–22) that his horse makes the fatal stumble; and see l. 1950 and note.

388. Man, like all created things ('creatures'), is, according to medieval theory, compounded of the four elements (earth, water, air, fire), as is the food he lives by. So Marlowe's Tamburlaine speaks of "Nature that framed us of four elements," and Sir Toby Belch (in *Twelfth Night*) asks: "Does not our life consist of the four elements?" The elements are sometimes pictorially represented as the materials of the Creation (*e.g.*, in Bartolo di Fredi's frescoes at San Gimignano, in Tuscany).

393–409. These lines are suggested by various passages in Boethius, though the sequence is altered:

God, whan he hath biholden from the heye tour of his purveaunce . . . doth swiche thing, of which thing that unknowinge folke ben astoned [Book IV, Prose 6] . . . some wenen, that sovereyn good be to liven withoute nede of anything, and travailen hem to be haboundaunt of richesses [Book III, Prose 2]. . . . Certes richesses han anoyed ful oft hem that han tho richesses ... [Book II, Prose 5; *cf.* Prose 4, *passim*] ... the corage alwey reherseth and seketh the sovereyn good, al be it so that it be with a derked memorie; but he not [=knows not] by whiche path, right as a dronken man not nat by whiche path he may retorne him to his hous [Book III, Prose 2].

396. Pollard aptly compares the passage in Juvenal that concludes:

> Nam pro jucundis aptissima quaeque dabunt Di.
> Carior est illis homo, quam sibi. ...

(For the Gods give what is most meet, not what is most pleasing. Man is dearer to them than he is to himself.)

(Satire X, 349–350.)

Parts (at least) of Juvenal were well known in the Middle Ages, and Chaucer may well have had these lines in mind.

401. *mateere.* Skeat interprets as 'the matter of thinking to excel God's providence.' With the following line he compares Romans viii, 26: "for we know not what we should pray for as we ought"; in that verse the implication is very different; but Chaucer may have had its phrasing in mind.

403. The simile is proverbial, being found in a delightful thirteenth-century poem in which a strayed reveller apostrophizes the Man in the Moon (No. 30 in *The Harley Lyrics*, ed. G. L. Brook, Manchester, 1948).

408. Boethius uses the term *felicitas* in Book III, Prose 2, where Chaucer translates it *welefulnesse.*

421–422. Boccaccio mentions only Arcita's fetters—when Peritoo takes them off. (*Tes.* III, 55.)

444. The wood of the (evergreen) box is described as 'yellow and pale.'

445. This apostrophe, or *exclamatio*, balances Arcite's musings in ll. 393–409. Again Chaucer is remembering Boethius:

> O thou governour, governinge alle things by certein ende, why refusestow only to governe the werkes of men by dewe manere? Why suffrest thou that slidinge fortune torneth so grete entrechaunginges of thinges, so that anoyous peyne, that sholde dewely punisshe felouns, punisheth innocents? ...

O thou, what so ever thou be that knittest alle bondes of
thinges, loke on thise wrecched erthes. (Book I, Metre 5.)
But he adapts the sentiments to the classical setting of the
tale by altering "O thou governour" to "O cruel goddes."

455–459. "What method or reason is there in a foreknowledge
which decrees that the innocent are tormented without
cause? My suffering is increased still more by the fact that
man, out of duty to God, is bound to keep the (moral) law,
and to give up the thing he wants."

In giving such questionings to Palamon and Arcite Chaucer
not only introduces one of his favourite topics but, by show-
ing them as brought by their grief to think about the lot of
men in general, adds depth to his characterization.

464. "There's no doubt that things may turn out thus."

470–471. Palamon accepts Arcite's view (*cf.* l. 232); but whereas
Arcite speaks of Saturn as a planet, Palamon refers to him as a
deity, like Juno. Juno, according to Statius, was angry with
Thebes because Jupiter her spouse had made love to Semele
and Alcmene there.

In the *Teseida* it is Arcita who refers to Juno's wrath
when talking with Peritoo after his release (III, 66).

486. *upon his heed*. A phrase modelled on the Old French '*sur sa
teste*'—'upon pain of losing his head.'

489. Such 'demandes d'amour' are common in medieval stories.
Boccaccio propounds them in his *Filocolo*, and Chaucer in the
Franklin's tale (F 1621 ff.). There is no evidence that such
questions were ever formally debated in 'courts of love,' as
once was thought, or that such courts ever existed.

496. *Explicit prima pars* . . . . This rubric, not proper to a
tale, was probably added, like those at ll. 1022 and 1624, by an
early scribe or editor. It occurs in the Ellesmere MS., but not
in any of the other important manuscripts, many of which do
not even leave gaps at these points.

503–520. This description of Arcite's plight is based on a similar
˷˷ in the *Teseida*, but Chaucer omits some details (*e.g.,*
effect of his unkempt beard) and adds others—
t; the references to his low spirits and mania.

According to medieval physiology, which was based on the works of Galen of Pergamum (A.D. 130–200), life depended on three spirits—natural, vital, and animal. The theory was that air passes from the lungs through the pulmonary vein to the left ventricle of the heart. Food substances are converted into blood by the liver, which endues this crude blood with 'natural spirit'—the power of growth and nutrition. Some of this crude blood is carried from the liver by the vena cava to the right ventricle of the heart. In the heart it mixes with the air from the lungs, and the mixture, being acted upon by the heat that is innate in the heart and remains there till death, results in a more refined, arterial blood, which, while in the heart, absorbs the principle of life in the form of 'vital spirit.' Some of this refined arterial blood, bearing vital spirit, reaches the brain (the seat of the soul—*anima*). There it generates the purest spirit of all—the 'animal spirit.' This animal spirit exists apart from blood and is carried by the nerves (thought to be hollow), through which it promotes motion and the higher bodily functions.

The brain is divided into three cells. The first or front cell is the seat of the 'Common' or unifying sense, as well as of the 'Fancy' ('phantasy,' *phantasia*)—the faculty by which objects are apprehended (a very different sense from the modern one). The middle is the seat of Reason, the third of Memory. The 'humours' (liquids governing the body and corresponding to the four elements) are carried through the body by the arteries. If evil humours reach the brain they engender manias of various kinds. The mania that is akin to the 'maladye of hereos' (515–516) and shares the same symptoms is engendered when the melancholic humour acts thus. It is the mania into which the desperate lover eventually falls.

The 'maladye of hereos' was a recognized medical description of the love-sickness from which Arcite suffers, its symptoms being lack of sleep and appetite, paleness, hypersensitivity, and, above all, swooning. Robert Burton, in his *Anatomy of Melancholy* (1621, etc.), has a long discussion of this 'heroicall love.' The phrase 'amor hereos' ultimately derives

from the Greek *eros* ('love'); but the spelling of some forms
suggests that when love began to be considered fitting to
a hero the word may have been confused with the Latin
heros. In medieval Latin *hereos* is found with the meaning
of desperate, passionate love. "Unless hereos is cured," says
de Gordon, "the sufferers fall into a mania, or die." (Bernard
de Gordon taught medicine in the University of Montpellier
in the early fourteenth century, and wrote the well-arranged
compendium, the *Lilium Medicinæ*.)

This belief in 'amor hereos' explains the uniformity of
lovers' behaviour as described in many medieval romances—
including Chaucer's own *Troilus and Criseyde*. But if Chaucer
makes his lovers conform closely to the conventional pattern
it is because he realized that the pattern was more than a
convention; it was based on human experience.

503. "He cannot sleep, and loses his appetite for food and
drink."

506. *Cf.* l. 444. The repetition of such conventional similes,
or of the conventional epithets of epic poetry (e.g., '*pius
Æneas*') was no blemish in poetry designed to be read aloud.
The listener absorbs the narrative more quickly if he can
accept without query some familiar descriptive phrases.

514. *geere* is probably 'behaviour, goings on' (*cf.* l. 673). But the
meaning 'clothing, attire,' equally well evidenced at this date,
would not be inappropriate for both *geere* and *habit* (520).
O.E.D. puts this instance of *habit* under the meaning 'mental
constitution, disposition,' but gives no other quotation illus-
trating that meaning earlier than 1579. Distraught lovers
have always neglected their appearance. Thus Hamlet, at the
time when Polonius thinks that he is suffering from "the
very ecstasy of love," has

> his doublet all unbrac'd,
> No hat upon his head, his stockings fould,
> Ungarter'd and down-gyved to his ancle,
> Pale as his shirt;   (*Hamlet* II, i, 76 ff.).

518. "In the front of his head, in the cell of Phantasy." The

reading in the text is based on MS. Harleian 7334. The Elles-
mere MS. reads "Biforn his owene celle fantastik," and most
MSS. agree with it in omitting *in*. If we keep *owene* it will refer
to *manie*—'its own cell'; mania being regarded as an infection
of the front cell.

527 ff. By introducing this vision of Mercury Chaucer again
links his characters with the gods more closely than Boccaccio
had done; though it is worth noting that Boccaccio's Arcita
when dying makes a moving prayer to this god (*Tes.* X, 94–
99). Mercury was giver of oracles and 'foreknower of the
fates.' His words have a delphic significance: Arcite's woe was
to end at Athens, to be sure; but at Athens he was also to die.

In describing Mercury and his sleep-bearing wand Chaucer
probably remembered the account in Ovid's *Metamorphoses*—
one of his favourite books—of Mercury preparing to slay
the hundred-eyed Argus, whom at Jupiter's command he first
lulled to sleep:

> Alas pedibus, virgamque potenti
> Somniferam sumsisse manu, tegimenque capillis.
> (I, 671–672.)

(He put on his winged sandals, took in his strong grasp the
sleep-producing wand, and donned his cap.)

He is generally represented as Ovid and Chaucer here
describe him—with cap (winged or flat), winged feet, and
bearing a magic wand (sometimes a herald's staff).

540. "I don't mind if I die, so long as it is in her presence."
Again the outcome gives an ironic significance to the words:
it is in Emily's presence that he does die.

550. This stratagem is not uncommon in the English popular
romances; and the phrasing of ll. 558, 564–567 is very similar
to that which such romances use to describe the young hero
who undertakes menial outdoor work and 'makes good.' It
would thus appeal to a miscellaneous audience, such as the
knight is supposedly addressing.

552. The squire—Chaucer's addition—perhaps represents the
faithful retainer of the romances.

570. In Boccaccio Arcita had changed his name to Penteo on leaving Athens. Philostrate is a curious adaptation of *Il Filostrato*, the title of the poem by Boccaccio on which Chaucer based his *Troilus and Criseyde*. It appears from his Proem that it was coined by Boccaccio from *philos* (love) and *stratus* (laid low).

588. Chaucer carefully indicates the passage of time. The number of years given here, taken with the periods of two years suggested in ll. 523 and 568, gives us the seven years of l. 594; whereas there is nothing to suggest that Boccaccio had more than the passage of a year or two in mind.

598. Chaucer, having asked "Who hath the worse, Arcite or Palamoun?" (490), is careful to present them as both equally afflicted with love-madness.

602. The religion of love had its martyrs as well as its saints (some of whom Chaucer had celebrated in his *Legend of Good Women*, which he himself called "The Legend of Cupid's Saints"). *Cf.* the 'pilgrimage' of l. 1356.

605. *The thridde night* is not specified in Boccaccio or elsewhere; the appeal to "olde bookes" is often made by medieval writers simply for emphasis, and may well indicate that the statement supposedly based on these books, is, in fact, new— as here.

The third night of May is presumably the night of the third of May; in which case Palamon and Arcite meet on the morning of the fourth. The special May observances, which Arcite has set out to perform (642), are, to be sure, generally associated with the first three days of May. But this is hardly sufficient reason for adopting Manly's view that the third night is the night *preceding* the third of May. He argues that the meeting was on May the third; that this date occurs on *some* lists of 'dismal' or inauspicious days; and that therefore we are to regard the meeting as unlucky. It is true that ill-luck befell Chanticlere, in the Nun's Priest's Tale, on Friday, May 3. But elsewhere (*Troilus and Criseyde* II, 56) Chaucer mentions "Mayes day the thridde" without connecting it with misfortune (unless Pandarus's love-longing is to be so considered). His reason for repeatedly specifying this date remains uncertain. (See also note, l. 679.)

614. There is no mention of drugs in Boccaccio (see p. 29), just as there is no mention of them in Ovid's story of Hypermnestra, though Chaucer, when adapting that story for the *Legend of Good Women*, again speaks of "narcotiks and opies" (2670).

O. F. Emerson (*Modern Philology*, XVII, 287) argued that opium from Thebes in Egypt is meant, since the country round about Egyptian Thebes was famous for its opium. But Chaucer's reference to Thebes here is surely derived from the description in the *Teseida* of the physician who, according to Boccaccio, helped Palemone to escape, as "nostro tebano" (V, 20) — that is, a fellow-citizen of the (Greek) city of Thebes. He may have thought that this was the Thebes whence the fine opium came.

619. *nedes cost.* This is equivalent to, and probably an adaptation of, the Old Norse phrase *nauthar kostr* ('dire choice').

621. "full of fear [caution] at every step." *Cf.* "with dredeful fot she sterte." (*Legend of Good Women*, 811).

635. Editors compare Dante, *Purgatorio*:

> la bel pianeta che ad amar conforta
> faceva tutto rider l'oriente. (I, 20.)

(The fair planet which hearteneth to love was making the whole East to laugh.)

But Dante's 'fair planet' was Venus, not Phœbus. Boccaccio, describing the May morning of l. 176, speaks first of Phœbus and then, in a phrase which suggests that he too had Dante in mind, of Venus, "per che il cielo rideva" (*Tes.* III, 5). While translating the *Teseida* Chaucer has been reminded by this phrase of Dante's more beautiful lines, which he has blended with Boccaccio's by substituting Phœbus for Venus, and applied to another May morning.

642. Chaucer adds these references to May and Maying, which he celebrates at greater length in the Prologue to the *Legend of Good Women*. Here they are in counterpoint to the opening

of the story: it is when Emily is doing her observance to May
that the lovers first catch sight of her (187–189).

643. "Always mindful of the object of his wishes"—namely, to
win Emily.

644. *startlinge as the fir.* Chaucer often adds this kind of simile to
his original (*cf.* "fiers as leoun," 740); he uses the same one
in describing the horse on which Æneas went hunting with
Dido (*Legend of Good Women*, 1204).

646. "it might have been a mile or two."

651. "with his face turned to the shining sun."

654. ll. 649–650 indicate that his garland is to be of green foliage
rather than of flowers "party white and rede" (as Emily's had
been seven years before; *cf.* ll. 195–196); and Manly sees a
specific allusion to the contests between the amorous orders
devoted to the flower and those devoted to the leaf—the sub-
ject of a fifteenth-century poem *The Flower and the Leaf.* But
l. 654 may mean that he hopes not only to make a garland for
himself but to be rewarded with one by his mistress. Medieval
love scenes (especially on ivories) often show a lady crowning
her lover with such a garland. It is worth noting that Chaucer
describes Emily when she enters the grove as "clothed al in
grene" (828).

663. *go sithen many yeres. Go* is a past participle (variant forms are
gon, (*y*)*go*(*n*); *ago*(*n*) was also a past participle in origin, from
the same verb-stem), and *sithen* an adverb, = 'before now.'
Translate: 'It was said many years ago, and is still true.'

664, 666. Chaucer has added these proverbial phrases. He
makes similar additions to his sources elsewhere—*e.g.,* 767–768,
and in the *Clerk's Tale* (which is based on Petrarch), 855 ff.:

> But sooth is said, algate I finde it trewe,
> For in effect it preeved is on me,
> Love is noght old as whan it is newe.

665–666. "It is a good thing for a man to keep an even
mind; for people are always meeting when they least expect
to" (literally, 'at an unappointed time,' and so 'by chance,
unexpectedly'). L. 666 is proverbial.

671. A roundel (or rondeau)—originally it accompanied a dance in a *ronde*, or circle—was a 12-, 13-, or 14-line poem built on two rhymes, the opening lines being repeated as a refrain. As in the example given by Chaucer at the end of his *Parlement of Foules*, Arcite's roundel would doubtless begin and end with the lines given in ll. 652–654, and that the first two of these lines would be repeated after l. 5 of the roundel. As the name suggests, the form was of French origin.

674. "Now at the top of the tree, now in the briars"—at the height of joy one minute, in the dumps the next.

679. Venus's day is Friday, *Veneris dies* (hence Fr. 'Vendredi'). Venus was equated with the Freyja of Scandinavian mythology, hence Old English *Friges dæg* (becoming 'Friday').

Attempts have been made to derive from the mention of Friday at ll. 676 and 681 an exact chronology based on the planetary days and hours (see p. 163), and even the year in which the Tale was written. Palamon and Arcite, it is argued, first meet on a Friday, because it is Venus's day; the duel takes place the next day (752); and the combatants in the tournament arrive on a Sunday exactly a year later (*cf.* ll. 992, 1330). But though Chaucer certainly gives precise astrological data in Part III, he gives none here. He does not state that Palamon and Arcite meet on a Friday, but quotes the proverb, 'Seldom is Friday like the rest of the week,' simply to illustrate his point that not only the mood of lovers, but everything else connected with Venus, is changeable. It is a waste of time to speculate whether Palamon and Arcite took the day appointed to be the Sunday on which the combatants reached Athens, the Monday given over to jousts and dances (1628), or the Tuesday of the final tournament (1633). Skeat, assuming that the "thridde nighte in May" (604) was the night of the third of May, took the day of the meeting to be the fourth of May, the day of the duel to be Saturday the fifth, and the year from that day to be the fifth of May in the following year—which would fall on a Sunday. The fifth of May did fall on a Sunday in 1381 and 1387; so Skeat, ruling out the first date as too early—and prior to the arrival of Anne of Bohemia, supposedly alluded to in l. 26—suggested that the tale was written in 1387. But all such argument assumes that the meeting is stated to have taken place on a Friday.

684 ff. This lament, or *exclamatio*, is blended from similar outbursts made at various times by both Palamon and Arcite in the *Teseida*.

708. "My death was ordained before my first clothes were made" (*i.e.*, 'before I was born'). Chaucer's lovers tend to be fatalists: thus Troilus appeals to the Parcæ as the

> fatal sustren, which, er any clooth
> Me shapen was, my destene me sponne.
> (*Troilus and Criseyde* III, 733–734.)

745. "Without assuredly dying at my hands." Cf. 819, "Without his being dressed."

765. "O Cupid, who art quite without [or regardless of] natural affection."

768. *Hir thankes*. One of the meanings of Old English *þanc* is 'goodwill.' Hence 'his thankes' means 'with his goodwill'; 'hir thankes,' 'with their goodwill' (and so, 'gladly').

780–790. Boccaccio (*Tes.* VII, 106) had taken this simile from a different context in Statius's *Thebaid* (IV, 494–499); but Boccaccio uses it to describe the emotions of the rival forces as they face each other at the tournament a year later. Chaucer makes some alterations, adds the effect of the beast crashing through the undergrowth (*breketh* is syntactically parallel with *hereth . . . thinketh*, but would be more naturally used of the beast), and expresses the hunter's thoughts in crisp, matter-of-fact phrases.

If we keep *hunters* in 780 (and the manuscript support for *hunters* and *stondeth* is strong), we must construe it as a genitive singular, dependent on *colour* (779), and translate: 'Just as the hunter's face [changes in colour as he hears the lion or bear approaching] . . . so these two went through changes in colour, inasmuch as each recognized the other to be his mortal enemy.'

791. Equally with l. 794, this line illustrates Chaucer's character-

istic response to the inherent pathos of the situation. He is sensitive to such pathos, but never harps on it.

798–801. The comparisons, like the overstatement of 802, are from the common stock of the romances. But Chaucer does not disdain to use conventional phrases when they serve his purpose. (*Cf.*, for example, l. 844.)

805 ff. The central thought of this passage (810–811) is found in Boccaccio; but, by relating it to the Boethian conception of destiny, Chaucer adds a philosophic dimension to the narrative: *cf.* Boethius, Book IV, Prose 6: "God disponith in his purveaunce . . . the thinges that ben to done, but he aministreth . . . by destinee, thilke same thinges that he hath disponed"; and *Troilus and Criseyde* V, 1541–44:

> Fortune, whiche that permutacioun
> Of thinges hath, as it is hir committed
> Through purveyaunce and disposicioun
> Of heighe Jove. . .;

and 984–985, *infra* (another addition by Chaucer).

820. The alliteration gives a vigour to this line quite different in effect from that of Boccaccio's stanza which it summarizes.

The picture of Theseus as a mighty hunter in this passage is virtually Chaucer's creation—one helped by his familiarity with the technical terms of the chase (*cf.* l. 836).

824. Diana being the goddess of hunting.

839. *Under the sonne*, "shading his eyes from the sun." We are to think of him as looking towards the east, in the early morning.

848 ff. By making Theseus (and not, as in the *Teseida*, Emily) discover the fighters, Chaucer speeds up the action and heightens the effect of surprise. In Boccaccio Teseo looks on for some time before asking who they are and expressing the wish, "May Mars give victory to him who most desires it." It is perhaps this phrase that prompts Chaucer to put into his mouth the oath (850) which sorts well with his impetuous character as suggested in the opening of the Tale (101 ff.).

888. Pollard suggests that the reference is to the cord used to tie

a man's hands behind his back when he was tortured by being jerked up and down over a pulley.

890. This scene, of Chaucer's devising (*cf.* p. 29), balances the opening scene of the Tale (53–103). There Theseus is quickly moved by the prayers of the kneeling women from mild annoyance to pity and from pity to anger. Here he is moved from anger to pity and from pity to perceptive self-mocking humour (of which there is only a hint in Boccaccio).

903. This line occurs no less than four times in Chaucer, the other instances being in the *Legend of Good Women*, F503, and the *Tales*, E1986, F479 (and *cf.* B660). The early Italian poets were equally fond of this sentiment (*cf.*, for example, Dante's *Inferno* V, 100), and Chaucer doubtless owed his phrasing of it to them. To say that he 'borrowed' it is not enough. His constant use of it helps to explain the attraction Italian poetry had for him; the poet who would excuse a repentant Criseyde "for routhe" (see *Troilus and Criseyde* V, 1099) found in such a line a mirror of his own feeling.

941. "Who can be a fool unless he love?"—"Your lover is your real fool."

952. The cuckoo and hare being traditionally stupid or mad (but the reading *of*, found in several MSS., may point to a lost proverb). It is characteristic of Chaucer that he savours a discussion of 'the miracles and cruel ire' of love with such a homely phrase (*cf.* 980). ('a gekgo or a swine' occurs in a similar context in Gavin Douglas's *Palice of Honour*.)

953. Probably, 'We all want to try everything once, no matter what it is'; *cf. Sir Gawain and the Green Knight*, 1844, "ever in hot and colde"—where the sense is clearly 'in all circumstances.'

956. *a servant*, of the God of love (*cf.* l. 1065), whose service is the theme of all courtly love poetry. Chaucer, who was soaked in this poetry, uses the term instead of Boccaccio's "innamorato" (*Tes.* V, 92).

969. Presumably they ask Theseus to take them under his lordship since, one being an escaped prisoner and the other liable to the death penalty (357), they have no legal status.

979. 'One of you, whether he likes it or not, may as well blow on an ivy leaf [to make it squeak], for all the good it will do him.' Chaucer uses the same phrase in speaking of Troilus's helpless plight (*Troilus and Criseyde* V, 1433).

983. *Degree.* Not (*pace* Pollard) 'this step of the ladder you want to climb,' but 'situation.' Cf. *Legend of Good Women*, 1031: "desclandred and in swich degre."

992. "A year from now, neither further nor nearer [*i.e.*, neither more nor less]" (Boccaccio, "un anno intero").

994–997. Boccaccio's Teseo speaks simply of a "battaglia nel nostro teatro" (*Tes.* V, 97). (*Cf.* p. 29.)

1007–1008. "You shall make no other settlement with me but that one of you shall be killed or captured."

1016. *Hath doon so fair a grace.* This somewhat unidiomatic expression is derived from the Italian "tanta grazia quanta fai" (*Tes.* V, 100). But see also s.v. Grace, sb. 8 in OE.D.

1027 ff. Chaucer (who as Clerk of the King's Works was himself responsible for the construction of the scaffolds for two tournaments at Smithfield in 1390) has modified a few of the details given in the *Teseida*, which speaks of 'marble walls' and over 500 tiers. He has added a north gate; and the oratories on the three gates are of his devising, though their decorative scheme includes details from Boccaccio's description of the house of Mars and the temple of Venus (see p. 30) and is influenced by the descriptions of the painted walls of Love's garden in the *Roman de la Rose* (ll. 140 ff. of Chaucer's translation).

1048. The reading in the text is found in only a few MSS. Ellesmere reads "And on the westward, in memorye"; Harleian, 7334, "And westward in the minde and in memorye." Such variants can be accounted for if we suppose that the copy or copies from which Ellesmere and other MSS. derive omitted *gate* accidentally, and that later copyists attempted to fill the gap as best they could.

1054. *Diane of chastitee.* Perhaps = 'Diana, goddesse of chastity' (*cf.* 1046); or 'the chaste Diana' (*cf.* "love of frendshipe" (= friendly love), *Troilus and Criseyde* II, 371, 962). But possibly *chastitee* is in apposition to *Diane*—'in honour of Diana that is, of chastity.'

1055. *doon wroght*, "caused to be made"; in modern idiom 'had made.'

1060. This is greatly abbreviated from Boccaccio's account, which Chaucer translated in full (with some slight alterations) in *The Parlement of Foules* (183–294). Both there and here he alters the list of 'love's folk'; here adding Narcissus (*cf. Romaunt of the Rose*, 1470 ff.), Solomon (a traditional type of the wise man made foolish by love), Medea, Circe, Turnus, and Crœsus; in the *Parlement* he adds Troilus, besides Tristram, Iseult, Achilles, Dido, Paris, Helen, Cleopatra, almost all of whom he would find in Dante's list of unhappy lovers (*Inferno*, V).

1066. "The oaths they swear in confirmation of their vows.'

1061–66. Boccaccio has no equivalent to these lines or to ll. 1089–94. Both here and in the parallel passage in the *Parlement* Chaucer emphasizes the sad and sinister effects of passionate love.

1075. No MS. gives a reading completely satisfactory in sense and metre. If we adopt Hg. the meaning will be: 'which I enumerated [when I saw them: *cf.* 1137] and propose to enumerate now.'

1078–79. Chaucer, like some other medieval writers, wrongly associates Venus (Cytherea) with Mount Cithæron (sacred to Bacchus and the Muses), whereas her legendary home was the island of Cythera.

1082. Idleness (Boccaccio's "Ozio") is the portress of the garden of love in the *Roman de la Rose* (538 ff. in Chaucer's translation).

1083. When Echo died of grief for Narcissus, who was inaccessible to love, Nemesis punished him by causing him to see his own image reflected in water; becoming enamoured of it, he pined to death.

1085. When Hercules fell in love with Iole, his wife Deianira sent him out of jealousy the poisoned shirt by which he died.

1086. Medea, in love with Jason, used her enchantments to

enable him to gain the golden fleece. Circe used hers against the companions of Ulysses; though he himself was proof against her magic he did yield to her love.

1087. Turnus fought Æneas for Lavinia, daughter of Latinus, and was killed.

1088. It is not clear why Crœsus, who was overthrown by Cyrus, should figure in this list.

1097. Chaucer has adapted Boccaccio's picture of the goddess herself (see p. 30) to fit his architectural design.

1112 ff. The ultimate source of this account—much of which is paralleled in Chaucer's *Complaint of Venus*—is the account in Statius's *Thebaid* (VII, 40 ff.) of Mercury's visit to Mars at Jupiter's behest. Boccaccio (*Tes.* VII, 29 ff.; *cf.* p. 30) personifies Arcita's prayer and substitutes it for Mercury. Statius sometimes seems to be describing images, sometimes real things; and there is similar uncertainty in Chaucer.

Some of the resounding words and phrases Chaucer owes to Boccaccio: e.g., *armipotente* (1124), *adamant eterne* (1132); but the grim instances of ll. 1160–62 and 1171–74 are his own; as are the references to the planet Mars (as distinct from the god) in ll. 1166 and 1179.

1129. *The northren light.* This can hardly be the aurora borealis, of which Chaucer probably knew nothing, but is rather 'the [weak] light such as one gets in the North.' The detail is perhaps suggested by Statius's account of Mercury "Arctoæ labentem cardine portæ"—'gliding down [to Thrace] from the gate of the Northern pole'; *Theb.* VII, 40); which is followed by:

> læditur adversum Phoebi jubar, ipsaque sedem
> lux timet.

('Phœbus's ray is weakened [when it strikes Mars' temple] and the very light fears that dwelling.' 45–46.)

1137 ff. (*Cf.* 1198 ff.) Contemporary listeners who kept in mind that it was a far-travelled knight who was telling the tale would find it easy to credit him with having seen what he here describes in the first person.

1152–53. Statius has "Tristissima Virtus stat medio" (51);
    Boccaccio (34), "e'n mezzo il loco la Vertu tristissima sedea."

1159. *shippes hoppesteres*. Statius has "bellatrices carinæ"; and
    Boccaccio, following him, "le navi bellatrici" (warships).
    Chaucer must have misread his copy of Statius or Boccaccio,
    or been misled by a bad spelling. *Hoppesteres* ('dancers')
    must be a translation of a Latin *ballatrices*, or an Italian *balla-
    trici*, neither of which is recorded. Chaucer evidently asso-
    ciated whichever form he read with *ballare* (to dance), under-
    stood the phrase to mean 'dancing ships,' and altered the
    conception from that of ships as symbols of war to that of
    destruction by fire ('brent').

1163. *by the infortune of Marte*. 'In regard to the ill-fortune
    wrought by Mars' (or, 'in regard to, *or* by, malevolent
    Mars'; though the use of *infortune* in the sense of 'an unfor-
    tunate or malevolent planet' is not clearly evidenced at this
    date).

1164. Boccaccio has (*Tes.* 37): "i vôti carri e li volti guastati"
    ('the empty chariots and mangled faces'); Statius (*Thebaid*,
    58):

    et vacui currus protritaque curribus ora,

    ('empty chariots, and faces ground by the chariots'). We
    should, therefore, probably render *carter* as 'charioteer';
    Chaucer uses the word in this sense in his translation of
    Boethius, and Gavin Douglas in his translation of Virgil
    (1513).

1166. *of Martes divisioun*. *I.e.*, subject to the astrological influence
    of Mars. *Cf.* Chaucer's *Complaint of Mars*, 272 ff.:

    But to yow, hardy knightes of renoun,
    Sin that ye be of my divisioun,
    Al be I not worthy so gret a name
    Yet seyn these clerkes I am your patroun.

1167. The barber figures here because in his medieval capacity
    as bloodletter he too "wields knives and sheds man's blood";
    the smith figures as the maker of swords, knives, and other
    weapons.

1177. *by figure*, the astrological diagram showing the aspect of Mars in relation to other bodies—presumably included in the paintings of the Death of Julius, etc.

1185–87. Puella and Rubeus were the names for two of the sixteen possible combinations that can be made by jotting down four rows of dots, when each row contains either one or two dots, thus:

.   .   .
.   Rubeus   .   Puella
.   .   .   .
.   .   .

Such figures were used in divination. Both Puella and Rubeus are sometimes assigned to Mars—Puella to Mars 'retrograd,' Rubeus to Mars 'direct.'

1189. The detail (Chaucer's addition) probably derives from the etymology of Mars (Mavors) found in the *De Deorum Imaginibus* of Albericus (*fl.* twelfth century) and possibly of still earlier origin. Albericus says that Mavors = 'mares vorans' (devourer of males—a description which might be applied to the wolf).

1198–1201. Diana, angered by the nymph Callisto's unchastity with Jupiter, turned her into a bear, and, according to one legend, later slew her in mistake for a real bear. Jupiter thereupon turned her into a constellation—usually identified with the Great Bear; but the lodestar is in the Little Bear.

1204–6. *Dane*. Daphne, daughter (according to Ovid; *Metamorphoses* I, 452) of Peneus, a river-god. Fleeing from Apollo, who loved her, she prayed for help and was turned into a laurel.

1207–10. *Attheon*. Actæon, who caught sight of Diana bathing and was turned by her into a stag, and then killed by his own hounds.

1212–14. *Atthalante*. Atalanta, a huntress averse to marriage, who, with Meleager, hunted and killed a wild boar that Diana had sent to ravage Calydon because Meleager's father Œneus had forgotten to sacrifice to her (see Swinburne's *Atalanta in Calydon*). Accounts of Meleager's later history vary; according to one, Aphrodite turned him into a lion for impiety. Chaucer apparently attributes Meleager's misfortune to Diana as in causing Atalanta to lose her chastity (Atalanta had a child by him, according to one story) he would anger Diana as goddess of Chastity.

1224. Diana was a 'diva triformis' (*cf.* l. 1455): Luna in heaven, Diana on earth, Hecate in Hades.

1225. Besides being a huntress and goddess of chastity, Diana was a friend and helper to women in childbirth. In this aspect she bore the name of Lucina, the goddess who makes the child see the light of day ('lucem').

1228. We can scarcely say that Chaucer has forgotten that he is describing a painted scene, for he reminds us of that in the next line. The painting is so vivid that the beholder might think he actually heard the woman in travail praying.

1242. *at alle rightes*—as Theseus had stipulated (994).

1244-47. "That, as far as knightly prowess was concerned, nowhere, since the world was created, had there ever been anywhere so fine a company for its size."

1257. *benedicite* ('bless us!') was probably here pronounced as a trisyllable: in a similar line in *Troilus and Criseyde* (I, 780) it is spelt *bendiste* in several MSS.

1263. *a paire plates large*. A protective covering worn over the habergeoun and consisting of metal splints riveted to a lining of fabric or leather; the breast-covering sometimes consisted of two large plates, buckled together; but the phrase refers to the whole covering.

This kind of armour can be clearly seen in the carving of a knight falling from his horse on a misericord in the choir of Lincoln Cathedral (South Side, no. 30).

Originally 'of' was not used after 'pair' (=set).

1264. The knight who had himself fought with the Teutonic knights of Prussia can fittingly introduce a reference to a Prussian shield, cf. *Prologue*, 53.

1270. In reducing Boccaccio's list of champions (which occupies the whole of Book VI of the *Teseida*) Chaucer has selected details from the descriptions of several of them and given them fresh application (besides adding some of his own) ; Thus Lycurgus's black beard, chariot, and bearskin with shining nails, in Boccaccio belong to Agamemnon (*Tes.* VI 22., *cf.* l. 36).

1284. *for-old.* *For-* has an intensive effect, as in Old English *for-oft.* The development was perhaps helped by the more common use of *for-* with past participles, implying completeness or destruction: e.g., *forfaded, forwithered, forroasted, forpined* (595). Cf. *for-blak,* 1286.

1298. Emetreus is a new character, invented by Chaucer, as might be suspected by his reference to the 'stories' (*cf.* note, l. 605). His crisp yellow hair (1308) and laurel garland (1317) belong in the *Teseida* to Peritoo (Pirithous):

> e biondo assai vie piú che fila d'oro,
> incoronato di frondi d'alloro.   (*Tes.* VI, 41.)

1300. Horses used in tournaments generally wore richly decorated caparisons reaching to the ground.

1302. *clooth of Tars.* A rich oriental silk, thought to have come from "Tarsia," apparently the name given to 'Turkestan.'

1342. Again Chaucer adds a detail which reminds us that it is the knight who had 'begun the board' in Prussia that is telling the tale; and the next three lines recall the description in the *Prologue* of the Squire, the Knight's son (95–100).

1344. The repeated reference to dancing is clumsy. Two MSS. read 'carole' for 'dauncen.'

1351 ff. Besides altering Boccaccio's order of the prayers (see p. 30) Chaucer has added details that give astrological significance to the times when they are made. The first 'unequal' hour after sunrise belonged to the planet governing the day (see p. 163). Palamon, getting up on Sunday night, two hours before sunrise (*i.e.*, two hours before the first hour of Monday) goes forth in the hour governed by Venus (1359), which planet is two before the moon in the planetary order. Emily gets up two hours later (*i.e.*, at sunrise, 1413–15) on Monday, the first hour of which is sacred to Diana, goddess of the Moon. *The nexte houre of Mars folwinge this* (1509) would be three hours later, the intervening hours being those of Saturn and Jupiter (Jove).

1357. See note, l. 1078.

1366. Adonis was beloved by Venus; at his death her grief was so great that the gods of the lower world allowed him to spend six months of each year with her.

1417 ff. In Boccaccio (*Tes.* VII, 71 ff.) the maidens, bearing "corni pien d'offerte," are sent to cleanse ("mondare") the temple and to prepare "le veste [the garments that Emila is to don after her ablutions] e'liquor [?the wine and milk later poured on the altar, for which Chaucer substitutes mead]." Then Boccaccio goes on:

Fu mondo il tempio e di bei drappi ornato;

(the temple was cleaned and decked with beautiful hangings); incense was burnt so that the temple was filled

di fummo assai soave in ogni lato.

(with sweet fragrance on every side); just as Palamon is said to have caused "ciaschedun tempio d'Attene fummare" (*Tes.* VII, 42).

It is usually assumed that 1423 is based on a misreading of 'Fu mondo' as 'fumando.' But the line may conceivably represent intentional abbreviation of Boccaccio's much longer account. For the 'absolute' construction *cf.* 2019.

1428–30. The sense seems to be: 'A full account would be delightful, and it would do no harm to the pure-minded; but it's best to let you imagine it for yourselves.'

1435. *dide hir thinges*, "performed her ritual." *thinges* suggests something formal and regular. *Cf.* "sey his thinges" (*Canterbury Tales*, B1281). The following line is a general reference to the kind of book in which one might find descriptions of such ritual in ancient times.

1444. *As keep me.* Chaucer several times uses *as* to introduce a request or prayer (*cf.*, for example, 1459). The use perhaps developed from such expressions as

> 'As wisly help me god the grete,
> I nevere dide a thing with more peyne.'
> > (*Troilus and Criseyde* II, 1230–31.)

('May god help me as surely [as it is true that] I never did a thing more unwillingly.')

1445. See note, l. 1207.

1491–92. Chaucer has transferred these phrases from Emilia's prayer in *Tes.* VII, 85:

> E se l'iddii forse hanno gi disposto
> Con etterna parola che e' sia
> da lor seguito ciò c'hanno proposto. . .

1497 ff. Chaucer has made an odd inversion. In the *Teseida* Diana's maidens appeared and spoke, and *then* one of the fires went out and re-lighted itself (signifying that one of the rivals would be defeated but would survive), while the second flowed with blood and went out (signifying that the other would die).

1575. Boccaccio's

> le cui armi risonaro
> tutte in sé mosse con dolce romore.
> e segni dierono al mirante Arcita
> che la suo orazion era esaudita. (*Tes.* VII, 40)

('whose arms . . . resounded with a pleasing noise . . .') has none of the implications of Chaucer's 'full low and dim'— nor the direct promise of victory.

1585. Saturn the planet is, as Gower says, 'cold in complexion,'

> and his condicion
> Causeth malice and crualte
> To him the whos nativite
> Is set under his governance.
> > (*Confessio Amantis* VII, 938–941.)

See also Appendix III.

1591. "One can outrun the aged but not better their counsel."

Chaucer, as usual, has added the proverbial stiffening.

1595. (*Cf.* 1810). *Doghter* may here be simply a term of affection-ate address used by the superior divinity (*cf.* 1490): Venus was the daughter of Jupiter (*cf.* 1364) the son of Saturn. But the *Roman de la Rose* (5541, 10827 ff.) would authorize Chaucer to refer to her as Saturn's daughter, as Lydgate does (*Reson and Sensuallyte*, 1460 ff.). Boccaccio simply says that 'a way was found to please both Venus and Mars' (VII, 67). He does not mention Saturn, and has no equivalent to ll. 1595–1620.

1596. *My cours*. The orbit of Saturn was the widest of any planet known in Chaucer's time.

1599. *the derke cote*. Perhaps the dark house in which madmen were confined.

1604. The zodiacal sign of Leo is opposite to the house or man-sion of the malignant Saturn, and Saturn's presence there made it still more malignant. Saturn's diurnal house was Aquarius.

1633. *on the morwe, i.e.*, on Tuesday, a day propitious for Arcite, since it was the day of Mars, to whom he had prayed for victory.

1644. *Knightes of retenue*, knights retained in the service of greater lords.

1658. The spectators point to, and discuss, their various 'favourites' in the coming tourney.

1667. A literal rendering of Boccaccio's "ancor le ricche camere tenea del suo palagio " (*Tes.* VII, 96).

1679 ff. In Boccaccio Theseus makes the proclamation himself. First in a long speech delivered some time before the day of the tourney (*Tes.* VII, 2–13) and then more briefly on the actual day (*Tes* VII, 130–132). By assigning the speech to a herald Chaucer emphasizes the kingly dignity of Theseus (*cf.* ll. 1671), which has no equivalent in Boccaccio. The condi-tions of ll. 1686–92 are new in Chaucer.

1703. A rendering of Boccaccio's "De' nobili e del popolo il romore toccò le stelle" (*Tes.* VII, 14).

The following lines are based on the account of Teseo's journey to the theatre *before* the day of the tourney (*Ibid.*).

1738. 'So that there should be no deception as to their number' (*i.e.*, to make sure that each side had exactly a hundred men).

1742. In these lines, set in balance against each other as the opposite sides are balanced, Chaucer suggests the rush and clang of combat partly by one- or two-syllabled words, and partly by alliteration, alliterative verse always being particularly effective in conveying the hurlyburly of battle (it was last used in medieval times in a poem on the battle of Flodden, 1513): Chaucer uses the same technique in describing the battle of Actium (*Legend of Good Women*, 640 ff.).

1749. Pieces of shattered lances spring twenty feet into the air.

1768. *Galgopheye* ('Gargapheye' in two MSS.), Gargaphia in Bœotia, where Actæon was turned into a stag. The association of this vale with hunting sufficed to suggest that it might be a natural home for tigers. Chaucer has adapted the simile from Boccaccio, who compares a combatant to a Hircanian lioness bereft of her whelp (*Tes.* VIII, 26).

1772. This comparison is added by Chaucer. The allusion to Belmarye comes aptly from the lips of the Knight, who had himself been there. Cf. *Prologue*, 57. Belmarye = Benmarin, an Arab province of N. Africa.

1805 ff. In Boccaccio Venus is in no doubt about the outcome, having already herself arranged for the appearance of the Fury from hell. The 'conceit' of ll. 1806–08 is Chaucer's; he uses it again in his *Envoy to Scogan*, stanza 2:

> By word eterne whilom was yshape
> That fro the fifte sercle, in no manere,
> Ne mighte a drope of teeres doun escape.
> But now so wepith Venus in hir spere
> That with hir teeres she wol drenche us here.

Mars had promised Arcite victory (1757)—but nothing more. But Saturn had promised Venus the fulfilment of her wishes (1619); and Arcite's complaint that his adversity was due to Saturn (230) is now tragically borne out.

1823–24. These lines are found in several MSS., but not in

the important Ellesmere, Hengwrt, and Cambridge (Gg. 4. 27) MSS. It would be rash to say that Chaucer did not write them; but if he did he may have cancelled them during revision. They are more Boccaccian than Chaucerian in sentiment, and scarcely sort with the character of the "parfit gentil knight." There is no exact parallel in the *Teseida*, though Boccaccio does say: "Let every man beware of falling unless he wishes to know who his true friend is. . . . He who was once loved is now abandoned" (*Tes*. VIII, 125).

1825. Several MSS. have *as* or *and* before *in*. Chaucer's original line may have been closer to Boccaccio's "l'animo suo sanza dimoro a lui voltò" ('her heart forthwith turned towards him'; *Tes*. VIII, 124), though he may have misread *voltò* as *volto* ('countenance'). A tentative reconstruction suggests itself:

And he was al hir cheere, and [*or* as] in hir herte.

('All her looks and feelings were set on him.')

1826. *furie*. Some MSS. read *fuyre* or some other spelling of 'fire,' which Pollard thinks may be right; but in the rubric to Book IX of the *Teseida* 'Erinis,' sent by Pluto, is described as "infernal furia," and Chaucer is doubtless following that rubric. True, Erinis breathes forth "le sulfuree fiamme," which might seem easier to acquiesce in than the appearance of a fury in person. But Chaucer is not troubled about probability at this point: concerned to be brief, he keeps the fury, but omits the flames, together with Boccaccio's description of their effect on the spectators (*Tes*. IX, 6).

1838. The detail is added by Chaucer and refers to the cutting of the laces and thongs by which various parts of the armour were tied together.

1852. *That . . . his*, "whose." In this line Chaucer is indicating the worst that befell any of the combatants. In Boccaccio's version several of them are killed.

1854. *charmes*, "magic spells." They would doubtless be used in conjunction with other remedies; thus the Old English charm against rheumatism was said while a salve was being prepared.

1855. *save*, "sage" (Latin *salvia*); highly valued in the Middle Ages as a medicinal herb. In the seventeenth century it is described as "a sovereign remedy for frenzy" and "good for venom or poison"; sage tea is still used as a stomachic and mild stimulant.

1856. *limes*. The Corpus reading *lives* is supported by several MSS., and by Manly, who argues that draughts are better adapted to saving 'lives' than 'limbs.' But in the fourteenth century 'limes' could be used of any part of the body.

1875 ff. Theseus proclaims that each side is equally eminent—another touch by which Chaucer enhances Theseus' character as an impartial judge—and distributes gifts appropriate to the rank of the combatants.

1885. Most of the medical details in this passage are added by Chaucer. Taken in conjunction with ll. 1833–35, they suggest that the injury Arcite received produced a clot of blood on or near the lung, and prevented the proper movement of the chest. Failure of oxygenation would produce the pain in the heart mentioned at ll. 1837, 1885–86.

1889. *veineblood*: blood-letting (by opening a vein)—a favourite medieval remedy. *ventusinge*: 'cupping'—the application to the skin of a cupping-glass in which the air is rarefied by heat, the blood being thus drawn away from the afflicted part. The cupping might be 'wet' (if the skin was scratched and made to bleed) or 'dry' (if the cup was applied without this scarifying). In dry cupping the glass is usually applied to the patient's back.

1891. According to Galenic theory (see note, 503–520), one of the functions of the animal virtue (='spirit') was to control the muscles, and in particular the respiratory musculature. The impurities in the blood that carried the natural spirit from the liver to the right ventricle were normally given off through the *vena arterialis* (the pulmonary artery) to the lungs, and thence exhaled. But if the lungs were damaged, so that they could not respond to the animal spirit's control, they could not perform this exhalation, and thus the conversion of natural spirit into vital spirit (in the heart) was hindered.

Chaucer seems to suppose that the clotted blood would produce poison and putrefaction; this would make the conversion of natural into vital spirit still more difficult.

1894. *Pipes.* Possibly 'veins.'

1895. The muscles of the lower part of the breast would be the
ones chiefly damaged by Arcite's sudden collision with his
saddle-bow.

1896. *corrupcioun*, "putrefaction," or possibly "pus" (though this
sense is not clearly evidenced before the sixteenth century).

1898. *Vomit.* Probably "emetic." *Cf.* Lanfranc's *Science of
cirurgie* (*tr. c.* 1400): "Laxatives and vometis ben nedeful to
hem that han olde rotid woundis." (This passage is quoted
as an example of the meaning 'emetic,' *s.v. Vomit, sb.* 4. in
O.E.D., which, however, gives the present line as an example
of the modern meaning.)

1901–02. Since life depended on the continual supply of
natural spirit, this spirit evidently became identified with
'nature' in the sense of 'the force by which the physical and
mental activities of men are sustained.' O.E.D., *s.v. Nature,
sb.* 10; *cf.* the quotation there given under the date 1541:
"[by bloodletting] nature dispensed over all the body is
lyghtened." O.E.D. gives no examples of 'nature' used in
contrast to 'physic' (in the general sense of 'medical skill
or treatment') before 1597; but it was doubtless a commonplace.

1903. *This al and som*, "this is the sum total, the long and the
short of it." 'This' is often equivalent to 'this is' in fourteenth-century English.

1917. In Boccaccio Arcita correctly addresses Emilia as
"cara sposa" (*Tes.* X, 66, 68) since they were formally
espoused after the tourney.

The impersonal simplicity of the following three lines is
very different in tone from the corresponding lament in the
Teseida; like the sudden turn to practical considerations in
the succeeding passages, it is characteristic of Chaucer (*cf.*,
for example, *Book of the Duchesse*, 209–220).

1928 ff. "And may Jupiter protect my soul as surely as [it is true that] I know no one in the world—as regards service in love, and all the behaviour particularly appropriate to that service—so worthy of love as Palamon."

Almost all the qualities listed in 1931–33 are those attributed to the Knight in the Prologue (43 ff.). They represent a considerable expansion of Boccaccio's "gentile e bello e grazioso." But in other respects Arcita's dying speech in the *Teseida* is much fuller (it occupies stanzas 101–111 of Book X), if less delicate.

1943. *And yet moore over*, "There is yet more to be said," "Nor is that all."

1945–47. Boccaccio puts it rather differently:

> sol nello 'ntelletto
> e nel cuore era ancora sostenuta
> la poca vita;
>
> (*Tes.* X, 112)

'Only in the intellect and in the heart was the little life sustained'—though a few lines later he speaks of Arcita as 'steadily failing [*'mancando'*] in his power'. Chaucer's lines yield a similar general sense, if we can translate: 'Very soon only the intellect, dwelling in his sick and painful heart, was left to fail, when the heart felt [the cold of] death.' (*Cf.* note 503–520). The ancient doctrine that the heart was the seat of the intellect was still current in the Middle Ages.

1950. Chaucer's substitute for Boccaccio's "A dio, Emilia." "Mercy, Emilye!" not only echoes Arcite's words when he first saw Emily (262–264), but gives point to ll. 1910–11.

1951 ff. *His spirit chaunged hous* is equivalent to Boccaccio's "l'alma sua aver mutato ospizio" (*Tes.* XI, 6)[1]; but the next six lines are wholly Chaucer's. In them he glances at the lengthy discussions by several medieval writers on the location of the

---

[1] The ultimate source doubtless being II Cor. v, 1: "Scimus enim quoniam si terrestris domus nostra hujus habitationis dissolvatur, quod aedificationem ex Deo habemus, domum non manufactam, æternam in cœlis." (*Cf.* Requiem Mass, Proper Preface, in the Roman Rite.)

soul after death. W. C. Curry cites a typical passage from
Duns Scotus's *De Anima Separata*: "The soul separated from
the body is within a certain limit somewhere or other pre-
sent. In this all agree, because it is not anywhere, nor is it
nowhere; and our faith is that the redeemed souls are in
heaven and the damned in hell." In the *Parlement of Foules*
(l. 30 ff.) Chaucer refers to the discussion of the problem in
Macrobius's Commentary on that part of Cicero's *Somnium
Scipionis* which he summarizes in the *Parlement* in the lines
beginning

> Thanne axede he if folk that here been dede
> Han lif and dwellinge in another place. . . . (50–51.)

(*Cf.* also *Legend of Good Women*, 18–20.)

  Boccaccio at this point describes the ascent of Arcite's soul
to the eighth heaven, from which, looking down at the little
globe where the mourners are still clustered round his body,
he condemns the blindness of mankind. This impressive
description Chaucer incorporates, with some slight changes,
into his account of the death of Troilus, at the end of *Troilus
and Criseyde*. In the *Teseida* Arcite goes "Theras Mercurye
sorted him to dwelle" (*Troilus and Criseyde* V, 1827; *Tes.* XI,
3): before his death he had sacrificed to Mercury and prayed
that he would transport his soul to Elysium. In the Knight's
Tale Chaucer for Mercury substitutes Mars, to whom Arcite
had prayed before the tourney. Boccaccio does not indicate
the ultimate destination of Arcite's soul. Indeed, any com-
ment on the fate of a pagan warrior would raise a hard ques-
tion for a medieval writer. Chaucer, while perhaps glancing
at Dante's *schema* in the *Paradiso*, where Mars is the planet
with which the souls of the brave are associated, has his narra-
tor make a frank and fitting admission of ignorance: it is not
for a knight to dwell on a question that troubles theologians.

1951–52. *ther as* = 'where.'

1954. "I find nothing about souls in the contents of my book."
  Pollard, following Liddell, interprets: "He does not find that
he has made any entry 'De Animis' in his table of contents

committing him to write about souls"; but the phrase may be purely metaphorical—'there is nothing in my undertaking that commits me to discussing souls.' It is less likely that Chaucer has in mind the contents of the *Teseida*, to which he never elsewhere refers.

1957. "May Mars guide his soul." Chaucer often introduces an optative clause with *ther*, the original sense of which, in this construction, may have been 'in that case,' or 'wherefore.'

1959. "No modern poet," says Manly, "would use such words as *shrieked* and *howled* in a serious passage like this"; but countless paintings suggest that the medieval mind did not regard loud and unrestrained expressions of grief as unsuitable for artistic representation (*cf.*, for example, Domenico Veneziano's Miracle of S. Zenobio in the Fitzwilliam Museum, Cambridge).

1964–68. These lines are new in Chaucer, who never passed lightly over women's sorrow. Ll. 1977–78 are likewise new. And in Boccaccio, Egeo (who is first mentioned as mourning along with many others) does not speak in *oratio recta*, or use the memorable image of 1989–90.

1977. *woldest* is here used in a weakened sense, and is practically equivalent to 'did': "Why did you have to die?"

2017. *a coroune of laurer grene*, Boccaccio's "frondi d'alloro." Chaucer's addition of *green* serves to remind us of the garland of green that Arcite set out to seek in the grove where he is now buried (649–653). Chaucer likewise puts a sword in the dead Arcite's hand, as if to remind us that on that same occasion (740) he had first drawn sword in the contest with Palamon that is now settled for ever.

2019. *bare the visage*. This construction is doubtless adapted from the French 'à visage descouvert.'

2037. *bowe Turkeis*. The 'arc Turquois,' to judge from other references to it, besides being of distinctive shape (Sancho Panza in *Don Quixote* describes himself as bent like a Turkish bow), usually had gold or silver mountings.

2056. *the service and the fir-makinge*. 'The funeral ceremonies and the building of the pyre.'

2060–2106. Perhaps the longest *occupatio* in English; it balances the briefer one with which the tale begins (see note, l. 17), and has a similar justification (*cf.* ll. 2107–8 with 27 ff.).

2102. Tyrwhitt (Chaucer's excellent eighteenth-century editor) says that "Chaucer seems to have confounded the Wake-plays, as they were called, of his own time with the Funeral Games of the Antients"; other editors have repeated this statement but none indicate what these 'wake-plays' were. *Pleyes* probably means no more than 'exercises, games, sports' (*cf.* Mandeville: "For joustinges, or for other pleyes and desportes"). If there be any confusion here it is between the two meanings of 'wake': (1) the watching over a dead body, (2) the annual festival of a parish church, kept up with dancing, wrestling, and other sports (such as Boccaccio describes in detail at this point).

2112. *Than semed me.* This unusual construction, in which *seem*, the impersonal verb, is used without *it* and followed by a dative (*me*) may be an imperfect rendering of Boccaccio's "parve" ('it seemed good') at this point, in a slightly different context (*Tes.* XII, 3). Translate: 'Then, it would appear.'

2129. *The first moevere.* In the scholastic philosophy of the Middle Ages (which was largely based on Aristotle) God is conceived of as the first mover, from whom all motion begins, descending from him through the Primum Mobile, the 'first moving' sphere, which in turn communicates motion to the other spheres.

By adding the phrase 'of the cause above' ('above' = in the heavens; *cf.* l. 1805) Chaucer has blended this conception with another scholastic conception—that of God as the first efficient cause, the original agency by which anything is produced.

2129–58. These lines are an amalgam of phrases and ideas found, in different order and context, in Boethius's *De Consolatione Philosophiæ* (*cf.* notes to ll. 76, 393 ff.). *Cf.* the following passages (here given in Chaucer's translation):

O thou, what so evere thou be that knittest alle boondes of thinges, loke on thise wrecchide erthes . . . fasten and ferme thise erthes stable with thilke boond by which thou governest the hevene that is so large. (Book I, Metre 5.)

That the world with stable feith varieth accordable chaunginges . . . that the see, gredy to flowen, constreineith with a certein eende his floodes . . . al this accordaunce of thinges is bounde with love, that governeth erthe and see, and hath also comandement to the hevene. . . . This love halt togidres peples joined with an hooly boond, and knitteth sacrement of mariages of chaste loves. (Book II, Metre 8.)

Thou bindest the elementis by nombres proporcionables, that the coolde things mowem accorde with the hote thinges, and the drye thinges with the moiste. (Book III, Metre 9.)

For the nature of thinges ne took nat hir beginninge of thinges amenused and inparfit, but it procedith of thinges that ben alle hole and absolut, and descendith so doun into uttereste thinges and into thinges empty and withouten fruit. (Book III, Prose 10.)

Thilke ordenaunce moveth the hevene and the sterres, and attemprith the elements togidre amonges hemself, and transformeth hem by entrechaungeable mutacioun. And thilke same ordre neweth ayein alle thinges growinge and fallinge adoun, by semblable progressions of sedes and of sexes.

(Book IV, Prose 6.)

2155. *progressiouns*; Boethius, *progressus* (pl.). "Sequences of productions" (?).

2169-72. "As regards mankind, too, we see that it is necessary that they die at one period or another—that is, in youth or age; the King and his servant alike must die."

For *nedeth* in l. 2170 some MSS. read *nedes*, 'of necessity,' which makes for a slightly easier construction.

The courtly reference in 2172 (as at 2226-27) is added by Chaucer.

2218. *parlement*. There is no mention of such an assembly or consultation in the *Teseida*. Chaucer has in mind the social and political aspects of marriage; in medieval times the marriage of a person of rank was bound to affect the common weal. Such a marriage is the theme of Chaucer's *Parlement of Foules*.

2225. "Give us an example of your womanly compassion."

2230. "That would have to be taken account of."

2231. "Mercy ought to prevail over justice." This language of courtly love is originally theological. Cf. *Legend of Good Women*, F160–162.

2246–48. The lines have no equivalent in the *Teseida*. With l. 2246 *cf. Cant. Tales* F. 792 ff. and with ll. 2247–48 *cf.* the ending of the popular romance *Havelok*:

> Nevere yete wordes ne grewe
> Bitwene hem, hwarof no lathe
> Mihte rise, ne no wrathe.
>
> (ll. 2975–78).

APPENDICES

Note. Line numbers refer to the Knight's Tale, except where it is stated to the contrary.

I. CHAUCER'S ENGLISH

THE language in which Chaucer wrote was basically that spoken by his London fellow-citizens. This may be thought of as a blend of the dialects of the near-by East Midland and south-eastern areas, with the East Midland element dominant; and it was already acquiring the prestige and importance that were soon to make it the standard literary language throughout the country—the 'King's English.'

Comparatively few words in Chaucer are completely strange to the modern reader; in vocabulary and syntax (though not so often in idiom) the language of his day was not essentially different from that which we now speak. The main difficulty for the modern reader lies in the changes of meaning that many of Chaucer's words have undergone. Sometimes the context offers a hint of such a change. Thus, when the Prioress's *conscience* is twice mentioned in connexion with her feelings for small animals we realize that Chaucer is here using *conscience* to mean 'tender feeling' rather than 'sense of right and wrong.' But it is not so easy to discover that *chivalrye* (Prol. 45) means not 'chivalry' in our weakened modern sense of 'courtesy,' but 'exercise of arms'[1]; or that the knight is described as *gentil* (Prol. 72) because he was well-born (185). Sometimes the meaning that a word suggests to a modern reader is still farther removed from Chaucer's intention.

Thus, *sadly* (1744) means not 'sorrowfully' but 'firmly'; *affeccioun* not 'love,' but 'feeling'; *solempnitee* not 'seriousness'

---

[1] At l. 7 of the Knight's Tale it probably has the still older meaning, of 'cavalry, knightly company.'

but 'due ceremony'; *vassellage* (2196) not 'servitude' but 'the actions of a courageous man'; and *imaginacioun* (236) 'fancy' or 'fantasy' (a sense still present in such phrases as 'It's all your imagination').

Even very simple words and phrases often cannot be adequately rendered by their equivalent modern forms. Thus *nexte* in the phrase *nexte way* (555) means 'nearest,' being an old superlative form; *wel ny* (549) means 'quite close at hand'; *al day* (666) means not 'all day' but 'every day, constantly'; *glide* (717) does not have the modern suggestion of smooth motion, nor *game* (1428) the modern suggestion of sport; *yvele* in such a phrase as "me list full yvele pleye" (269) cannot be rendered as 'evilly'; it simply gives a negative force to the verb ('I am not inclined to joke'). *Slepy* (529) refers to the *soporific* power of Mercury's wand. Occasionally a word is used in the literal sense of its Latin original; *e.g.*, an intricately plaited garland is described as *subtil* (L. *subtilis* 'finely-woven').

Finally, in a few words the resemblance between an old and a modern form is misleading (*a*) because the two have no connexion: e.g., *wisly* (1005) is not an adverbial derivative of *wis* 'wise,' but of *gewiss* 'certain'; *him thoughte* (96) ('it seemed to him'; *cf.*, 'methinks') is of different origin and meaning from 'he thought'; or (*b*) because the word has gone through several changes in application: e.g., *to wedde* (360) means 'in pledge' (the verb *to wed* = 'to marry' having reference to the particular pledge involved in marriage); *to borwe*, with the same meaning (Old English 'borg' = a security), has a similar relation to the verb *to borrow* (which originally implied 'to borrow on security').

Changes in the meaning of other words (including such common verbs as *shall* and *will*) are indicated in the Glossary; and in general it will be worthwhile to consult the Glossary—unless the meaning is self-evident—whether a form is familiar or not.

The relation between the language that Chaucer wrote and the Old English (or 'Anglo-Saxon') spoken and written in England before the Norman Conquest, can be clearly traced The chief differences are in vocabulary and inflexion.

Vocabulary

Much of Chaucer's vocabulary, and many of the idioms and constructions he uses, had been adopted either from literary French or from the form of French spoken in England from the Norman Conquest till his own day. Sometimes a French word or phrase had superseded an English one, sometimes it had blended with it: *e.g.*, L. *sanctus*, O.E. *sanct*, O.Fr. *saint*; the adoption of the latter was at least rendered easier by the existence of the O.E. form. *Bi cause* is an example of an English phrase modelled on a French one (*par cause (de)*); and such phrases are important evidence of the fusion of the two languages—a fusion which resulted, among other things, in a rich variety of doublets (e.g., *remedye ne reed*, 358).

Chaucer was not necessarily the first to adopt or adapt the French words and phrases first recorded in English form in his writings, though his prestige doubtless often gave them wider currency than they would otherwise have enjoyed; but some (e.g., *dien in the peine* (275), *on his heed* (486) — cf. Fr. *mourir en la peine*, *sur sa teste*) are not found outside his poetry.

A few words and phrases are of Norse origin. They were introduced into the language by the Scandinavians who settled in the Danelaw and elsewhere, and sometimes ousted their English cognates. Thus *boone* 'prayer' ousts O.E. *bēn*, and *they* O.E. *hie*. Amongother Scandinavian adoptions are *felawe* and *fro*.

Inflexions

The complex system of Old English inflexions had become greatly simplified by Chaucer's day; the main inflexional differences between his language and that of the Authorized Version of the Bible being that in native English words a final -*e* or -*en* or -*es*—which usually represents a 'levelling' in unstressed position of Old English word endings in -*e(n)*, -*a(n)*, -*o(n)*, -*u(m)*—still survives in Chaucer, with the grammatical value of the particular inflexion from which it was derived. Thus, *alle*, pl. (85, 86) is descended from O.E. *(e)alle*, *eallum* (dat. pl.); *eyen*, pl. (925) from

O.E. *eagan*, dat. pl. *eagum*; *houndes*, pl. (89) from *hundas*; *leeve* (278) from *leofa*; and *asshen* from the 'weak' plural *ascan*.

As inflexions disappeared their function was taken over by prepositions. But there are traces of an intermediate stage, where distinctive inflexion has gone, but a preposition was not felt to be necessary; e.g., *a trewe man*, dative = 'to an honest man' (468); = O.E. *anum treowum menn*.

Nouns. The genitive singular ending -*an* of the O.E. 'weak' noun was no longer used, but the corresponding 'strong' genitive ending in -(*e*)*s* had not yet been substituted in all such nouns. Hence *the sonne upriste* (193)—'the rising of the sun'— O.E. *sunnan*.

Certain O.E. nouns had no distinctive flexion in the genitive singular or nominative or accusative plural. Thus in *fader soule* (Prol. 781) *fader* represents O.E. gen. s. *fæder* (cf. *brother*—O.E. gen.s. *broþor*; 2226); and O.E. plural forms *hors*, *ʒear*, and *þing* appear in Chaucer as *hors*, *yeer*, and *thing* (*cf.* Prol. 644, 736; K.T. 2178).

Face (779) represents an Old French plural form.

Sustren (161) has acquired a 'weak' plural ending since the Old English period (cf. *children*; O.E. pl., *sweostor, cildru*).

Adjectives. In Old English a 'weak' form of the adjective was used after the definite article, the demonstrative pronoun, and sometimes after possessives. The endings of these 'weak' adjectives survive as –*e*: e.g., *this hoote fare* (951).

Sometimes an adjective follows the French order: e.g., *humour malencolic* (517); and the same sequence is found when neither noun nor adjective is of French origin (*stalke grene*, 178); and even when the adjective is separated by a phrase from its noun: e.g., *fettres on his shines grete* (421); *opie of Thebes fine* (614).

Pronouns. *Ye* (nominative) is still kept distinct from *yow*, (accusative), as in the Authorized Version. *His* is the gen. s. form of (*h*)*it* as well as of *he*. The plural forms are:

> Nom: *they*
> Acc: *hem*
> Gen: *hir(e)*; *her*

(The forms *they, their, them*, are of Norse origin, and first appear in areas of Norse influence.)

Hise (pl. adj.) is a new formation in Middle English on the analogy of the *pl.* forms *mine, þine*.

[In *it am I* (602, 878) *it* is a predicative pronoun, representing the person meant. The modern 'it is I' results from *it* being later regarded as the subject, and the person of the verb altered to agree with it.]

VERBS. The main differences between the forms used by Chaucer and those of the Authorized Version are:

Infinitive. The O.E. ending in *-an* is sometimes preserved as *-en*: *letten* (32).

Present Indicative. A 'contracted' third singular occurs in *rit* (116)=*rideþþ*. The plural often ends in *-en*: *we witen* (402).

Past Indicative. The O.E. plural ending in *-on* often survives as *-en*: *losten* (78). *Highte* (2, 699) is a relic of an old passive form; it is used with both past and present meaning.

Imperative. The plural form in *-eth* (O.E.-*aþ*) occurs often (e.g., *herkneth*, 985).

Past Participle. The past participle of an O.E. 'strong' verb had, besides a distinctive ending, in *-en*, a prefix *ge-*; *-en* survives in Chaucer's language as *-e* or *-en*; the prefix often survives as *y*, but sometimes disappeared entirely. Hence a great variety of forms: e.g., *wonne* (6), *y-drawe* (86), *shapen* (708).

Verbs adopted from French took the ending of the O.E. weak past participle—in Chaucer usually written *-ed*: e.g., *asseged* (23).

THE SUBJUNCTIVE. The subjunctive or 'conceptual' mood was still in living use in Chaucer's day, and not restricted to formal use and to a few set phrases, as in modern English. Examples are in lines 250 and 353. But even in O.E. some subjunctive forms were indistinguishable from their indicative equivalents; and so in Chaucer *hadde* (O.E. *hæfde*) represents either Past Ind. (e.g., 345) or Past Subj. (e.g., 372).

IMPERSONAL CONSTRUCTION. Impersonal constructions are far more common than in modern English: e.g., *al be him looth or lief* (979), *semed me* (2112), *him liked* (1234), *it ran him* (544). *Men*

(= man, 'one') is used as an impersonal subject, with a singular verb: e.g., *What asketh men to have* (1919).

PERFECT TENSE. The verb *have* is used with a past participle to form a 'perfect tense,' as in modern French. This tense is usually equivalent to an ordinary past tense in modern English: e.g., *hath slain* (144), *han torn* (162).

For illustrations of the changes in force and meaning of the verbs *can, coude, may, shal, sholde, wil, wolde*, see the Glossary. A verb expressing motion is sometimes implied after *wil, wolde* (*e.g.*, 399).

Spelling and Pronunciation

The spelling conventions current in Chaucer's day were based in large measure upon the Old English spelling system, which had been on the whole phonetic—each letter had represented a distinct sound. French scribal customs had modified, without altogether upsetting this system. By the fourteenth century two new methods of indicating long vowels were in general use:
(1) *e* and *o* were doubled; $\bar{u}$ was represented by *ow* or *ou* (a specifically French practice):
(2) *-e* following a single consonant had come to be regarded as a mark of length; contrast *blake* rhyming with *make* (41–42), and *blak* rhyming with *spak* (53–54).

The phonetic value of the long and short vowel sounds was probably as follows:

> Short *a, e, i, o, u* as in French *patte*, English *pet, pit, pot, put*. *a* after *w* had the same sound as in other positions. *Cf.* the rhyme at 553–4. Long *a, i, u*, as in English *rather, ravine, rude*.

> Long *e* had either the 'close' sound of the final *-e* of French past participles (e.g., *frappé* [ē], or the 'open' sound of the vowel in English *fair* [ɛ̄]. Words that originally had the close sound are usually nowadays spelt with *ee* (e.g., *meet, green*). Words that originally had the open sound are usually nowadays spelt with *ea* (e.g., *heath, great*). Long *o* had either the open sound of the vowel in *oar* [ɔ], or the close sound of the vowel in French

eau [ō]. Words that originally had one of these sounds
are usually nowadays spelt with *oo*, *oa* respectively (e.g.,
good, *boat*).

y is merely a spelling variant of *i*.

au (in *straunge*, *remembraunce*, etc.) probably represents the
sound [ɔ] still used in such modern words as retain
this spelling (e.g., *paunch*, *vaunt*).

Final *-e* was generally pronounced, but not (except 'in
pause') before another vowel, or in certain plural pro-
nominal forms (*hise*, *hire*, *oure*, *youre*, *thise*).

As in Old English, all *consonants* (except initial *h*-, in words
of French origin) had phonetic value. Thus, initial *w*- (before *r*)
and *c*- *k*- (before *n*) were still pronounced; and words ending in
-ight did not rhyme with words in *-ite*. *-l-* was pronounced before
f, *k*, *m*, (*half*, *folk*, *palmer*). *-r-*, as in Modern Scots, was pro-
nounced in all positions (*mordrour*).

II. A NOTE ON THE METRE

The Knight's Tale, like the Prologue and most of the verse
Tales, is written in rhymed couplets, the lines usually contain-
ing ten syllables[1] and five stresses. Chaucer was the first to
use this measure in English verse, and he modelled his line, in
part, on the French decasyllabic line. But French verse lacked
the stress-accent that gives Chaucer's lines their characteristic
rhythm; in a typical Chaucerian line the stresses fall as follows,
with regular alternation between the stressed and unstressed
syllables:

But we biséken mércy and socóur (60)

The line usually opens with an unstressed syllable followed by
a stressed one. But sometimes the initial unstressed syllable is
omitted:

Ó persóne allóne, with-óuten mo, (1867)

---

[1] Disregarding the final unstressed *-e* at the end of a line and 'in
pause.'

or the order of the initial stressed and unstressed syllable is inverted:

Bright was the sónne, and cléer that mórweninge (204)

(when this pattern is repeated for several lines it gives an effect of activity and excitement, as in ll. 2500-11, 2602-15). And occasionally the line opens with a three-syllabled 'foot':

Up springen spéres twénty fóot on highte (1749)

Reading a passage aloud will show that the distinction between stressed and unstressed syllables is not always very marked Prepositions, conjunctions, and auxiliary verbs are not usually susceptible of heavy stress, and a line composed chiefly of such words may have only two or three clear stresses:

Er it were day, as was hir wóne to dó (182),[1]

On the other hand, a stressed syllable is sometimes followed immediately by one bearing the same or almost the same stress ('secondary stress'):

Of brénd gòld was the cáas, and éek the harnéis. (2038)

Words of French origin usually retained the stress on the last syllable of the stem: *natúre, prisoún, senténce, soldás, contrée.* (So *mateére,* rhyming with *héere,* 401–402). But the English tendency to place the stress on the first syllable was already affecting such words, so that we also find *séntence, cóntree* (in 11, as against *contrée,* 6).

Proper names were particularly liable to variable stress: e.g., *Arcíte,* 222, *Árcite,* 78; *Átthenes,* 3; *Átthenés,* 22 (*perhaps* = 'Athenians').

In polysyllables of French origin the third syllable generally seems to carry weaker stress than the first: *avèntùre, pílgrimàge.* This is also true of polysyllables with the English suffixes *-inge, -nesse: hoóm-comìnge* (26), *hévynèsse* (2200).

[1] In *were, wone, -e* would be 'silent.'

In such forms as *tales, olde, wonne, hadde, ycleped, servise,* the final *-e, -es, -ed,* normally has syllabic value in Chaucer's verse (though it may not always have been preserved in ordinary speech); a rhyme like *Rome/to me* (Prol. 671–672) would be possible only if *Rome* was disyllabic. But in certain plural pronominal forms (*hise, hire, oure, youre, thise,* and sometimes *whiche, some*) the final *–e* was regularly silent.

In such words as *hevene, owene, evere,* the *e* preceding the *n/r* was apparently slurred (*e.g.,* 2247); but *sey(e)n* 'to say' was often disyllabic (*e.g.,* 1028).

i has syllabic value in *-ioun,-ience* (*e.g., pacience,* 226; *composicioun,* 1793); and sometimes in the endings *-ie, -ye(s),* representing Latin *-ia(s)* (*fermaciës,* 1855).

Final *-e* is regularly elided—except when it occurs 'in pause' (*i.e.,* before a cæsura)—before a vowel or 'silent' *h*; and final *-o,* in unstressed position, elides similarly:

Ne I ne axe nat to-morwe to have victorye (1381)

But note the lack of elision in 'ne oinement . . .' (Prol. 631).[1]

Sometimes Chaucer uses an alternative form of a verbal inflexion in order to avoid this elision of *-e*: e.g., *to seken him* (510), as against *to seke* (17).

The necessities of rhyme also force him to use such alternative forms as *if it may been* (52) as against *it may noon oother be* rhyming with *adversitee* (227–228). For the same reason he occasionally uses a South-Eastern dialect form instead of its more usual East Midland equivalent: e.g., *him leste* (145–146) rhyming with *reste,* as against *hire liste* rhyming with *upriste* (193–194).

We have every reason to believe that Chaucer had a 'good ear'—probably a better one than the scribes of any of the extant manuscripts, who were liable, in Chaucer's own phrase, to 'miswrite' or 'mismetre.' But in the decasyllabic couplet he was experimenting with a new metre; and in view of the volume of his work, and the speed at which some of it must

[1] In many positions *-e* was probably very lightly pronounced, or slurred.

have been written, it is inevitable that a few lines should have
been left awkward or defective.

But if we read Chaucer's verse aloud—and he expected it to be
read aloud—we shall not often be troubled by these difficulties.

III. ASTROLOGY AND ASTRONOMY

When we see the sun each day rise in the east, go up the sky
to the south, and set in the west, we take it for granted that its
movement is merely apparent, and that it is the earth we stand
on that is actually moving and revolving like a top once a day
while the sun stays still. But in the Middle Ages it was held that
the earth was stationary and that the sun went round it.

If we observe the stars night after night we see that, though
they do not move in relation to each other, the whole of the
heavens appears to move once a night, like the sun, from east
to west. This apparent motion is again attributable to the fact
that the earth we stand on is revolving. In the Middle Ages it
was held that all these stars were equidistant from the earth and
were fixed in a sphere which revolved about the earth at its
centre once every day.

We now know that the varying seasons of the year are due to
the movement of the earth in its annual orbit about the sun.
In the Middle Ages it was held that they were due to the move-
ment of the sun about the earth. But this movement was not the
same as the daily one already mentioned; it was a second and
annual movement. The sun, like the stars, had a sphere, and it
moved about the earth in it. A medieval schoolmaster might
have illustrated it in this way. Take a round ball in your hand,
put a ladybird on it, and set her walking in one direction. Turn
the ball round on its axis like a top in the opposite direction.
When you have turned the ball completely round once the lady-
bird will have done two things. First, she will have travelled
round with the ball, and secondly, she will have walked a small
distance in the opposite direction. The ladybird is the sun, the
ball is the sphere of the sun; the first movement of the ladybird

is the daily movement of the sun round the earth, and the second is part of the annual movement. Suppose that after three hundred and sixty-five revolutions of the ball the ladybird has walked once completely round it in the opposite direction. That is the number of days in the year, the time it takes the sun to go once round the earth from west to east. The daily motion is, of course, from east to west.

The sun, however, according to medieval theory, did not make its annual journey in the reverse direction along exactly the same line as its daily journey. It made it in an orbit inclined to the plane of its daily journey at $23\frac{1}{2}°$, thus:

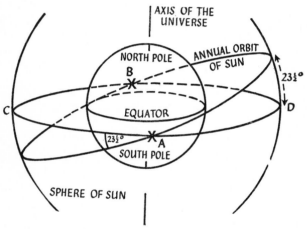

A and B are the equinoctical points, and the points A, B, C, and D are in the plane of the equator and of the daily movement of the sun about the axis of the universe.

We now know that this angle of $23\frac{1}{2}°$ is truly accounted for by the fact that the axis of the earth is tilted at this angle from the perpendicular as it goes through its orbit about the sun.

Suppose it is spring, and you are observing day by day that the sun rises farther east and at noon is higher in the sky. You are observing the effects of its annual 'journey.' If you imagine this annual orbit drawn on the sky and imagine the stars behind it—for they are there, and it is only the brilliance of the sun that puts them out—you will find that it is drawn approximately over twelve groups of stars, vaguely resembling certain objects and creatures like (though not including) the well-known Plough and Orion. Fill out the line of the annual orbit of the sun to a broad band either side of it to include the whole of these groups, and that is the 'zodiacal circle.'

The twelve groups occupy twelve equal parts of this band, the 'Zodiac,' and each part is called a sign and is named after the constellation in it. The signs are: Aries (the Ram); Taurus (the Bull); Gemini (the Twins); Cancer (the Crab); Leo (the Lion); Virgo (the Virgin); Libra (the Scales); Scorpio (the Scorpion); Sagittarius (the Archer); Capricornus (the Goat); Aquarius (the Water-carrier); and Pisces (the Fishes). See p. 162.

Since there are twelve signs and twelve months in the year the sun takes about a month to get through each sign. It starts at the beginning of the first sign, the Ram, on March 12, a date equivalent to our March 21 (the difference in date is due to an error in the earlier calculations). This is the Spring Equinox, when day and night are of equal length (see A and B in preceding diagram). On this day spring begins. Since it takes a month to get through each sign it does not leave the Ram until the middle of April, and thus it spends half of each sign in one calendar month, and half in the next.

	RAM		BULL		TWINS	
MARCH		APRIL		MAY		

Most stars do not alter their positions in regard to each other, and were therefore called 'fixed' stars; but some heavenly bodies do, *viz.*, the planets, which we now know go round the sun like the earth, but which the Middle Ages held went round the earth like the sun. They too moved in spheres, and these were concentric about the earth and increasingly distant from it in the order Moon, Mercury, Venus, Sun, Mars, Jove, Saturn.

Like the sun, they had two motions, one daily from east to west, and one from west to east of duration varying from planet to planet. Medieval people regarded the orbits of the planets, traced on the sphere of the fixed stars, as, like that of the sun, within the belt of the Zodiac.

Two things should be remembered: first, the earth is entirely motionless in the centre, and secondly, the spheres are invisible, only the planet moving in each being seen. The system can be visualized as a Chinese puzzle where a number of boxes are contained inside each other. It is called the Ptolemaic System and was generally received until the seventeenth century when the discoveries of Copernicus led men to conceive of the planetary system in somewhat the same way as we do now.

It was believed in the Middle Ages that all things in this earth and generally below the sphere of the moon, were *influenced*, though in the Christian view not *determined*, by the stars and planets. The planets, for example, had each an individual influence. Jove disposed a man to cheerfulness, sobriety, kingliness, peace, and prosperity. Thence we derive our word 'jovial.' (*Cf.* 'mercurial,' 'saturnine,' etc.) The original use of the word *influence* in English was for this 'flowing in' of astral power.

Each sign of the Zodiac had a particular 'influence,' and this was especially important when the sign was 'in the ascendant'—that is, just appearing on the eastern horizon. The influence of a sign modified the influence of any planet passing through it. Each planet had its own special 'house,' or sign, and when in it, as it circled through the Zodiac on its journey around the earth from west to east, it exercised a specially strong influence. This was even greater when the sign was in the ascendant, and the planet in it was then called the 'lord' of the ascendant.

Each planet and sign influenced a particular part of the body, as Chaucer wrote in his treatise on the 'Astrolabe' (the medieval predecessor of the sextant): "Aries hath thin heved, and Taurus thy necke and thy throte, Gemini thin armholes and thin armes."

The relations of the planets to each other in the sky (their 'constellation,' or 'aspect') also modified their influence, and

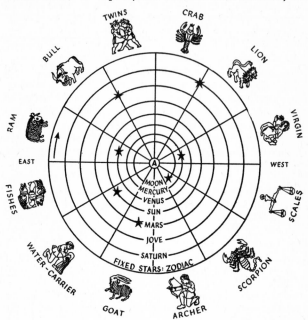

The earth is at the centre of this diagram. Imagine yourself to be Mr A standing on it out of doors. Look to the eastern horizon (along the line to 'East' in the diagram) and you see that the Ram is the ascendant sign—i.e., just appearing above the horizon. (The arrow indicates the direction in which you will see the heavens appear to move if you watch long enough: the direction, that is, in which the spheres move daily.) Venus is in the ascendant sign. Let your eyes travel directly upwards, overhead, and then down to the western horizon. You will have passed through the signs in the top half of the diagram. Saturn and Jove you will have seen in 'sextile.' You will not have seen the other half of the heavens because it is under the earth.

these relations were partly classified according to the angle sub-
tended between them at the earth. Thus two planets were in
'opposition' when 180° apart, in 'trine' when 120° apart, in
'quartile' when 90°, 'sextile' when 60°, and in 'conjunction'
when together.

Each day of the week was specially dominated by one of the
planets, Sunday by the Sun, Monday by the Moon, and so on.
The day from sunrise to sunset was divided into twelve parts,
and so was the night from sunset to sunrise. The twenty-four
hours thus determined were necessarily unequal except at the
equinoxes (when day and night are equal). According to one
theory, the first hour after sunrise belonged to the planet
governing that day, and thereafter each hour in turn was
assigned to the next planet in order, beginning with the most
distant from the earth and working inward.

A prognostication of the destiny likely to be enjoyed by any
person involved calculations about most of these factors as they
stood at the moment of birth. A physician had to assess these
influences when treating a disease, since the different parts of
the body and the different diseases were dominated by different
stars.

IV. A GUIDE TO WIDER READING

SKEAT, W. W. (editor): *The Works of Geoffrey Chaucer*, 6 vols.
(Oxford University Press, 1894). Notes and glossary espe-
cially good.

ROBINSON, F. N. (editor): *The Complete Works of Geoffrey
Chaucer*, (Oxford University Press, 1957). Notes an excellent
guide to detailed works on particular points. Glossary in-
different.

DRYDEN, J.: *Preface to the Fables* (1700).

KER, W. P.: *English Literature: Medieval* (Home University
Library, 1912, 1945).

KITTREDGE, G. L.: *Chaucer and his Poetry* (Oxford University
Press, 1915, 1951).

LEWIS, C. S.: *The Allegory of Love* (Oxford University Press, 1936).

LOWES, J. L.: *Geoffrey Chaucer* (Oxford University Press, 1934).

COGHILL, N.: *The Poet Chaucer* (Home University Library, 1949).

RICKERT, E. (compiler): *Chaucer's World* (Oxford University Press, 1948).

TILLYARD, E. M. W.: *The Elizabethan World Picture* (Chatto and Windus, 1943). (Medieval and Elizabethan beliefs about the structure of the universe had much in common.)

TREVELYAN, G. M.: *English Social History*, illustrated edition (Longmans, Green and Co., 1950). Vol. I.

GLOSSARY

THE glossary is intended to be not a concordance but a record of such words and phrases as have changed in form or meaning since Chaucer's day. Minor changes in spelling are disregarded.

Only the first instance of a word or meaning is given. When variant spellings occur, the line reference is to whichever form occurs first.

A list of abbreviations used will be found after the Contents.

Before using the glossary, read the Appendix on Chaucer's English and especially its warning to beware of words that look the same as modern words but have now changed their meaning. Read also the note at the beginning of the Y letter-group.

A, on (cf. **Amorwe**); in, 2076.
Abiden, *v.*, wait (for), 69; *p.p.* 2124.
Abood, waiting, delay, 107.
Aboute, around, 1275; in turn, 32; **been a.,** go about, be scheming *or* preparing, 284.
Above(n), above, in the heavens, 741, 1805; in the upper part, 1045.
Abregge, *v.*, cut short, 2141.
Aboughte, *pt. s.*, suffered, 1445; **aboght,** *p.p.*, paid for, 2242.
Accomplice, *v.*, accomplish, 2006.
Accord, agreed plan, 2224.
Acorded, *p.p.*, agreed, 356.
Accused, *p.p.*, censured, blamed, 907.
Aday, in the day, 1765.
Adoun, down, 132; below, 2137.
Aferd, *p.p.*, afraid, 660.
Affeccioun, emotion, feeling, 300.
After, afterwards, 131; according to, 1715; **a. oon,** alike, 923.
Again, Ayein, again, 34; in return, 339; in reply, 234.
Again, Ayein(s), against, 929; towards, 1822; see note, l. 651.
Agaste, *pt. s. refl.*, was scared, 1566; **agast,** *p.p.*, terrified, 1483.
Ago(on), *p.p.*, gone away, 418; gone by, 1926; passed away, 924; gone out, dead, 1478; see **Yore.**
Aiel, grandfather, 1619.
Al, all, 16; everything, 2175; **alle,** pl., 54; **a. and some,** every one, all, 1329; **a. and som,** the sum total, 1903.

Al, *adv.,* quite, entirely, 814; *conj.,* although, 313; 2141.

Alaunts, mastiffs, 1290.

Al day, constantly, 310; continually, all the time, 522; every day, 666.

Alighte, *pt. s.,* arrived, alighted, 125; **alight,** *p.p.,* 1331.

Alle, see Al.

Allegge, *v.,* cite, quote, 2142.

Als(o), also, 439.

Alway, always, 492.

Amadrides, Hamadryades, wood-nymphs, 2070.

Amenden, *v.,* improve (on), 1338; reform (ourselves), make amends, 2216; correct, put right, make amends (for), 2208; *p.p.,* 52.

Amiddes, in the midst, 1151.

Amorwe, on the next day, 763.

Amounteth, *pr. s.,* means, 1504.

An, on, 207.

Anclee, ankle, 802.

Angwissh, severe suffering of body or mind, 172.

Anight, at night, by night, 184.

Ano(o)n, straightway, at once, 113; **right a.,** right away, 107.

Apaid, *p.p.,* satisfied, contented, 1010.

Apalled, *p.p.,* dimmed, weakened, 2195.

Apparaillinge, preparation, 2055.

Appeere, *v.,* appear, 1488.

Appetit, desire, bent, inclination, 812.

Aretted, *p.p.,* imputed, 1871.

Arm-greet, as thick as one's arm, 1287.

Armes, arms, armour, 16; **in oon a.,** in the same (kind of) armour, 154; coat of arms, 2033.

Armipotente, powerful in arms, 1124.

Array, dress, 'get-up,' appearance, fitting arrangement, position of matters, condition, 76.

Arrayed, *pt. s.,* prepared, fitted out, arranged, 1232; *p.p.,* dressed, 531; **be they noght wel a.,** what a fine appearance they have, 943.

Arre(e)st, detention, 452; rest (for spear), 1744.

Ars metric, arithmetic, 1040.

Art, pursuit, occupation, 1933.

Artow (= art thow), 283.

Arwes, arrows, 1108.

As, as, 1; **a. now,** at present, 27; **a. for me,** as far as I am concerned, 761; **a. a knight,** in knightly array, 754; **as** (introducing *imp.*), see note, l. 1444; **a. out of that contree,** as regards that country, 487.

Ashamed, *p.p.*, put to shame, humiliated, dishonoured, 1809.

Aslaked, *p.p.*, diminished, 902.

Asp, aspen, 2063.

Aspect, relative position of the planets as supposed to influence things on earth, see note, l. 229.

Assaut, assault, 131.

Assayed, *p.p.*, tried out, experienced, 953.

Asseged, *p.p.*, besieged, 23.

Assemblen, *v.*, assemble, 428.

Assent, consent, accord, 2111; opinion, 2217; **by noon a.,** on any terms, 87.

Assente, *v.*, agree (to), 2234.

Assh (1), ash-tree, 2064.

Asshen (2), *n. pl.*, ashes, cinders, 444.

Assureth, *pr. s.*, keeps stable, makes secure, 68; **assuren,** *pr. pl.*, confirm, 1066.

Asterte, *v.*, escape, 737; **astert,** *p.p.*, 734.

Astoned, *p.p.*, astonished, amazed, 1503.

At-rede, *v.*, surpass at counsel, out-wit, 1591.

At-renne, *v.*, surpass at running, out-run, 1591.

Aett (= **at the**), 263.

Atthamaunt, adamant, 447.

Atthenes, Athens, 3.

Auctoritee, author *or* book having title to be believed, 2142.

Auter, altar, 1047.

Ava(u)ntage, advantage, 435.

Aventure, chance, fortune, (chance) event, accident, (trial of) chance, 216; hazardous undertaking, 430; **min a.,** what happened to me, 302.

Avis, consideration, opinion, 1010.

Avow, vow, 1379.

Axe, *1 pr. s.*, ask, 489.

Axing, request, 968.

Ay, always, 325.

Ayein(s), see **Again.**

Bacheler, probationer for the honour of knighthood, 2227.

Bad, *pt. s.*, bade, 528.

Balled, bald, 1660.

Bane, cause of death, 'death,' 239; slayer, 823.

Barein(e), barren, devoid of, 386.

Barre, bar, 217.

Bataille, battle, 21.

Bauderye, gaiety, jollity, 1068.

Bay, bay-coloured, 1299.

Be(en), be, 52; **be,** *pr. s. subj.,* 243; *1 pr. pl.,* 66; *p.p.,* 65; **been,** 1 *and* 2 *pr. pl.,* 47.

Beere, bier, 2013.

Beete, *v.,* kindle, make up, 1395.

Benedicite, *exclam.,* praise [the Lord], bless us, 927.

Benigne, kind, gentle, meek, 1357.

Bente, field, slope, 1123.

Berd, beard, 1272.

Bere, bear, 782.

Bere, *v.,* bear, conduct (oneself), acquit (oneself); carry, 564; **bere,** *pr. s. subj.,* 1689; pierce, 1398; **ba(a)r,** *pt. s.,* 322; **ber,** *imp.,* 1902; **(y)born, (y)bore,** *p.p.,* borne, born, 120; **he bar him lowe,** behaved like a humble person, 547; see note, l. 665.

Beste, for the b., as intended for the best, 989.

Bettre, better, 396.

Bibledde, *p.p.,* covered with blood, 1144.

Bide, *v.,* wait, stay, 718.

Bifalle, *v.,* happen, 947; **bifel, bifil,** *pt. s. impers.,* (it) happened, 151.

Biforn(e), before, in front (of), 1105.

Biginne, *v.,* begin, 34; *pr. s.,* 2160; **bigan,** 1 *pt. s.,* 496; *pt. s.,* 690; **bigonne,** *p.p.,* 1315.

Bihote, 1 *pr. s.,* promise, 996.

Bijaped, *p.p.,* tricked, 727.

Biknowe, *v.,* acknowledge, 698.

Binde, *v.,* bind, 1556; **bond,** *pt. s.,* 2133; **(y)bounden,** *p.p.,* 291.

Binding, bond, 446.

Biraft, *p.p.,* taken away (forcibly), 503.

Biseken, 1 *pr. pl.,* implore, 60.

Biset, *p.p.,* arranged, ordained, 2154.

Bisy, busy, diligent, 633; anxious, restless, 1462.

Bisynesse, business, diligence, care, 1070; **diden b.,** took pains, worked industriously, 149.

Bitwix(en), between, 22.

Biwreye, *v.,* reveal, 1371.

Blak(e), black, 41.

Bleinte, *pt. s.,* started back, 220.

Blisful, blessed, enjoying the bliss of earth or of heaven, 1357.

Blisfully, joyfully, enjoying earthly bliss, 378.

Blisse, happiness, 372.

Blive, quickly, 1839.

Blood, race, lineage, 472; kinsman, 725.

Blowen, *pr. pl.,* blow, 1654; *p.p.,* proclaimed; **b. up and doun,** spread abroad, 1383.

Bocher, butcher, 1167.

Bokelinge, *prp.,* buckling, 1645.

Boket, bucket, 675.

Boles, bulls, 1281.

Bond, see **Binde.**

Boon, bone, 319.

Boone, petition, prayer, 1411.

Bore, Born, see **Bere.**

Borwe, pledge, **leid to b.,** pledged, 764.

Bouk, trunk, body, 1888.

Bounden, see **Binde.**

Bowes, boughs, 784.

Brak, see **Breke.**

Brawnes, muscles, 1277.

Bratful (=bretful), brimfull, 1306.

Brede, breadth, 1112.

Breke, *v.,* break, 96; *pr. s.,* 784; **brak,** *pt. s.,* 610; **broken,** *p.p.,* 310.

Breme, furiously, 841.

Brenne, *v.,* burn, 2009; *pr. s.,* 1546; **brenne,** *pr. pl.,* 1473; **brendest,** 2 *pt. s.,* 1526; **brente,** *pt. s.,* 1545; **brenden,** *pt. pl.,* 1567; *prp.,* 1142; **(y)brent,** *p.p.,* 88; **brend,** *p.p.,* that has been refined by fire, 1304.

Brenninge, burning, 138.

Breres, briars, 674.

Brest, Brist, breast, 442.

Bresten, *v.,* break, 1122; **brest,** *pr. s.,* bursts, 1752.

Briddes, birds, 2071.

Bridel, bridle, 46; **hast . . . al the b. in thin hond,** are the leader *or* controller, 1517–1518.

Bringe(n), *v.,* bring, conduct, 755; *pr. subj.* (let no man bring), 1687; *pt. s.,* 11; **(y)broght,** *p.p.,* 253.

Brist, see **Brest.**

Brode, broad, 1278.

Broided, *p.p.,* braided, 191.

Brondes, pieces of burning wood, logs, 1480.

Browdinge, embroidery, 1640.

Bulte, *pt. s.*, built, 690.

Burned, *p.p.*, burnished, 1125.

Buskes, bushes, 721.

By, by, through, at, in, beside, etc., 20; **b. and b.**, next to each other, 153; **b. the cause,** because, 1630.

Cas (1), chance, happening, 216; case, 278; matters, (state of) affairs, 553.

Cas (2), quiver, 1222.

Caitif, captive, miserable, wretched, 694.

Caitives, (piteous) wretches, 66.

Calle, *v.*, cry out to, 1227.

Cam, *pt. s.*, came, 125.

Can, *pr. pl.*, *etc.*, recognize, know, know how, are able, are skilled (in), 396; **c. . . . thank,** shows gratitude, expresses thanks, 950; **coude,** *pt. s.*, *etc.*, 512.

Cantel, portion, piece, 2150.

Care, anxiety, sorrow, trouble, 463.

Careful, sorrowful, 707.

Careine, corpse, 1155.

Carieden, *pt. pl.*, carried, 2042.

Caroles, ring dances to the accompaniment of a song, 1073.

Carte, chariot, 1164.

Caste, 1 *pr. s.*, reckon, 1314; *pt. s.*, cast, 38; considered, pondered, 1996.

Castes, contrivances, 1610.

Cembd, *p.p.*, combed, 1285.

Cerial, belonging to a species of oak, 1432.

Certes, certainly, 17.

Certein, particular (but unspecified), 613; fixed, definite, 2135; a certain number of, 2109; certainly, 281.

Cervere, carver, 1041.

Chaar, chariot, 1280.

Chamberlein, officer of the household in charge of the bed-chamber, 560.

Chambre, room, bedroom, 207.

Champartye, equality; **holde c.**, share in power, 1091.

Charge, care, responsibility, **yevest litel c.**, don't worry much about, don't lose sleep over, 2 *pr. s.*, 426; (moral) weight, importance, **it were no c.**, it would be of no importance, 1429.

Charitee, love, **out of alle c.**, full of resentment, 765; benevolent act, act of kindness *or* fairness, 575; **seinte c.**, holy charity, 863.

Chastein, chestnut, 2064.

Cheere, Chiere, behaviour, manners, demeanour, 1361; look, expression of face, 55.

Chees, *imp.*, choose, 737.

Cherles, *gen. pl.*, of the peasants, of the rude mob, 1601.

Chieftain, commanding officer, captain, 1697.

Chiere, see **Cheere.**

Chirking, grating, strident noise, 1146.

Chivalrye, feats of knightly valour, 7 (it is not always clear when the sense is this or the next); cavalry, company of knights, 20.

Circuit, circumference, 1029.

Circumstaunce, ceremony, formality, 1405; relevant detail, 1930.

Citole, stringed instrument, played by plucking, 1101.

Citrin, lemon-coloured, greenish-yellow, 1309.

Clariounes, shrill, narrow-tubed trumpets, 1653.

Clarree, sweet drink of wine, honey, and spices, 613.

Clateren, *pr. pl.*, rattle, 1501; **clatereden,** *pt. pl.*, 1565.

Clause, shortly in a c., in a short space of time, 905.

Cleer, bright, fair, clear, 204.

Cleere, clearly, brightly, 1473.

Clepen, *v.*, call, name, 1872; **(y)cleped,** *p.p.*, 9.

Clerk, man of learning, 305.

Clothered, *p.p.*, clotted, coagulated, 1887.

Cockow, cuckoo, 952.

Col-blak, black as coal, 1284.

Cold(e), cold, 444; gloomy, dispiriting, cheerless, 1062.

Cole, coal, 1834.

Colered, having collars, 1294.

Colpons, bits, pieces, 2009.

Commune, in c., generally, commonly, 393.

Communes, common people, 1651.

Compaignye, party, 40; intercourse, 1453.

Compas, circle, 1031.

Compassing, devising, contrivance, 1138.

Compleinte, (love) lament, 2004.

Complexioun, disposition, 'make-up,' 1617 (the 'blend' of 'humours' in a person).

Composicioun, agreement, contract, 1793.

Concluden, *v.*, sum up, summarize, 500; draw a conclusion, 2209.

Conclusioun, decision, judgement, 885.

Condicioun, character, disposition, 573.

Confort, comfort, succour, 390.

Conforteth, *pr. s.,* comforts, 100.

Confus, bewildered, perplexed, 1372.

Confusioun, ruin, destruction, 687.

Conseil, counsellor, confidant, 289; **of my c.,** in my confidence, 283; council, 2238; **to my c. sworn,** bound by oath to keep my confidence, 725.

Conserve, *imp.,* preserve, 1471.

Constellacioun, grouping of the heavenly bodies as supposed to influence things on earth, see Appendix III, 230 (L., *con* (*cum*) = together, + *stellatus*=set with stars).

Contek, quarrels, strife, 1145.

Contenaunce, appearance, 1058.

Contrarye, opponent, 1001.

Contree, country, region, 6.

Convoyed, *pt. s.,* escorted, 1879.

Convertinge, *pr. p.,* turning back, 2179.

Corage, heart, spirit, 1087.

Coroune, crown, garland, circlet, 1432.

Correccioun, correction, punishment, 1603.

Corrumpable, corruptible, 2152.

Corve(n), *p.p.,* cut, 1839 (the laces of the armour were cut).

Cosin, cousin, 223.

Cote, cottage, 1599 (see note).

Cote-armures, vests worn over the armour and bearing heraldic devices, or 'coats of arms,' 158.

Couched, *p.p.,* laid, 2075; beset, studded, 1303.

Coude, see **Can.**

Cours, orbit, 1596; action of coursing, *or* hunting with hounds, **han a c.,** pursue (with hounds), 836; charge, bout, 1691.

Courser, horse for coursing, *i.e., either* galloping in hunt *or* bearing knight in battle, 846.

Couthe, *pt. s.,* could, 1014.

Covenants, promises, resolves, vows, 1066.

Cracchinge, scratching, 1976.

Crafty, skilful, 1039.

Creature, human being, 43 (anything created), 389.

Crope, top of a tree, 674.

Cry, clamour, importunate calling, 42.

Crye, *v.,* cry out, 237; **2** *pr. pl.,* 50; **crid(e),** *pt. s.,* 220; **cride(n),** *pt. pl.,* 91; **cridestow,** didst thou cry out?, 225. See **Lete.**

Cure, care, attention, 1995; **diden c.,** applied (themselves) diligently, 149.

Dampned, *p.p.,* condemned, 317.

Dar, 1 *pr. s.,* dare, venture, 293; **darst,** 2 *pr. s.,* 282.

Darreine, *v.,* vindicate *or* decide a claim to, 751; maintain (battle) in vindication of a claim, 773.

Daun (a title of respect like *Mr*), 521; (Like *Don* and *Dom*, < L. *domnu*='master').

Daunger, influence, power, **withouten . . . d.,** under no obligation, without supervision, 991.

Daweth, *pr. s.,* dawns, 818.

Debonaire, meek, gentle, 1424.

Decree, ordinance, **and swich d.,** and all such formal enactments, 309.

Dede, see **Deed.**

Deduit, pleasure, 1319.

Deed, dead, 264; like death, 720, **dede,** *pl.,* 84.

Deedly, deathly, like death, 55.

De(e)l (part, bit), **every d.,** wholly, 967; **never a d.,** not one jot, 2206.

De(e)re, dear, 376.

Deeth, death, 106.

Defye, *v.,* repudiate, 746.

Degree, rank, order, station, 310; position, situation, 983; step, 1033.

Deide, *pt. s.,* died, 1988.

Deis, dais, 1342.

Delit, pleasure, delight, 821.

Deme, *v.,* judge, consider, 1023; **demeth,** *imp.,* 495.

Departe, ., part, separate, *pr. s. subj.,* 276; **departen,** 1 *pr. pl.,* 2212.

Depe, deeply, solemnly, 274.

Depeint(ed), *p.p.,* depicted, 1169.

Dere, *v.,* harm, trouble, 964.

Derre, more dearly, **hath d.,** loves more, 590.

Despence, Dispence, spending, expenditure, 1024.

Despit, malice, anger, 83; **in d.,** to show his contempt, 89.

Despitous, contemptuous, 738.

Desplayeth, *p. s.,* unfurls, displays, 108.

Destreineth, see **Distreine.**

Devise (of), *v.,* tell, describe, 136; devise plan, 396; ordain, direct, 558.

Devoir, duty, one's best, 1740.

Deye, *v.,* die, 2176.

Diapred, *p.p.*, bearing diaper patterns, 1300.

Diched, *p.p.*, having a ditch or moat, 1030.

Dide(n), see **Do(on),** 251.

Dight, *p.p.*, prepared, 'got ready,' 183.

Digne, worthy, 1358.

Diligence, I shal doon d., I shall carefully see to it (that), 1612.

Dim, faint, indistinct, 1575.

Dirke, dark, evil, foul, 1137.

Dirriveth, *pr. s.*, is derived, 2148.

Dis, dice, 380.

Disconfitinge, defeat, 1861.

Disconfiture, defeat, 150.

Disconfort, grief, annoyance, 1152.

Disconforten, *v.*, dishearten, grieve, 1846.

Disjoint, 'disjointed condition,' **in no d.,** without getting in a 'fix' *or* in difficulties, 2104.

Dispence, see **Despence.**

Dispitously, scornfully, angrily, sharply, 226.

Disposicioun, position of a planet modifying its astrological influence 229, see Appendix III; disposal, control, 1506.

Disserved, *p.p.*, deserved, 858.

Distreine, *v.*, hold in its grasp, afflict, 958; *pr. s.*, 597.

Divininge, *prp.*, guessing, forecasting, 1657.

Divinis, divines, theologians, 465.

Divinistre, one with power to see into the future, 1953.

Divisinge, skilful provision, 1638.

Divisioun, distinction, 992; see note, l. 1166; disagreement, discord 1618.

Dominacioun, power, 1900.

Dongeoun, tower, keep, 199.

Do(on), *v.*, do, perform, cause, make, exert, 84; **do(o)th,** *pr. s.*, 141; **doon,** *pr. pl.*, 673; **dide(n),** *pt. pl.*, 319, 149, see **Bisynesse;** **(y)do(on),** *p.p.*, 167; **hath d. make,** caused to be made, had made, see 1047, cf. 1055; **of ydon,** put off, doffed, 1818.

Doute, out of d., without doubt, certainly, 283.

Dowves, doves, 1104.

Drawe(n), *v.*, draw, carry, recall (to memory), 558; *pr. s. subj.*, let (no man) draw, 1689; **ydrawe(n),** *p.p.*, 86.

Drede) fear, 538.

Drede, 1 *pr. s.*, dread, fear, 735

Dredeful, cautious, 621, see note.

Drenching, drowning, 1598.
Dresse, *pr. pl.*, range, draw up, 1736.
Dreye, dry, 2166.
Drope, drop, 62.
Drugge, *v.*, drag, **to d. and drawe,** to fetch and carry, 558.
Duk, ruler, 2.
Duetee, homage, reverence, 2202.
Dure, *v.*, remain, last, 378.
Dusked, *pt. pl.*, grew dim, 1948.
Dwelle(n), *v.*, dwell, remain, 115.

Ech, each, 274; **e. after oother,** one behind the other, 41.
Echon, each one, 1797.
Eek, also, 13.
Eet, *pt. s.*, ate, 1190.
Effect, effect, issue, outcome, substance, 331, 1370.
Eft, again, 811.
Eileth, *pr. s.*, ails, 223.
Eir, air, 388.
Elde, (old) age, 1589.
Elles, Ellis, else, otherwise, 293.
Emforth, in proportion to, according to, **e. my might,** as far as in me lies, 1377.
Empoisoning, poisoning, 1602.
Emprise, undertaking, enterprise, 1682.
Encens, incense, 1571.
Encombred, *p.p.*, **e. of,** burdened with, 860.
Encrees, increase, 1326.
Encresseth, *pr. s.*, increases, 457; **encressen,** *pr. pl.*, 480.
Ende, end, 534; upshot, result, 986; end of debate, conclusion, agreement, settlement, 1007; **your e.,** end of your dispute, 1011.
Endelong, along, lengthways, 1133.
Endite, *v.*, write, compose, put into words, relate, tell of, 351.
Engendred, *p.p.*, born, produced, 517.
Enhauncen, *v.*, advance, raise, 576.
Enhorte, *v.*, exhort, 1993.
Enoint, *p.p.*, anointed, 2103.
Ensample, example, illustration, 1181.
Entente, intention, purpose, 142; **in good e.,** with good will, 100.
Er, before, 182; **e. that,** before, 1498.
Eres, Eris, *pl.*, ears, 664.

Ere, *v.*, plough, 28.

Erles, great noblemen, 1324.

Erst, e. than, before, 708.

Erthly, mortal, 308.

Eschue, *v.*, escape, avoid, 2185.

Ese, ease, 111.

Esen, *v.*, help, comfort, relieve, entertain, 1336; *p.p.*, 1812.

Espye, *v.*, catch sight, descry, 254; discover, discern, 562.

Esta(a)t, Staat, estate, rank, state, condition, 68.

Estres, apartments, inner rooms, 1113.

Ete, *v.*, eat, 89.

Eterne, eternal, 251.

Even(e), just, impartial, 1006; equal, 1730; in a steady, balanced way, 665; exactly, **e. joinant,** right up against, 202.

Everemo, for ever, 371.

Everich, each one, 328.

Everichon, every one, 1737.

Ew, yew-tree, 2065.

Executeth, *pr. s.*, carries out, 806.

Eye, eye, 38; **eyen,** *pl.*, 925; **seen at e.,** perceive at a glance, 2158.

Fader, father, 1611.

Fadme, fathoms, 2058.

Fair(e), *adj.*, beautiful, excellent, desirable, 13; considerable, 1016.

Faire, *adv.*, well, 'nicely,' elegantly, properly, 1433; according to plan, 126; **f. and wel,** in proper manner, 968.

Falle(n), *v.*, fall, happen, 810; *pr. s. subj.*, 1697; **fel, fil,** *pt. s.*, 176; **fille(n),** *pt. pl.*, 91; **fille,** *pt. subj.*, should fall, 1252; **(y)falle,** *p.p.*, 1845.

Falow, pale, grey, 506.

Fantastic, pertaining to phantasy, see note, ll. 503–520, 518.

Fare, behaviour, 'goings-on,' 'ado,' 951.

Fare(n), *v.*, behave, act, fare, go, 537; 1 *pr. pl.*, 403; **ferde,** *pt. s.*, 514; **ferden,** *pt. pl.*, 789; **fare,** *p.p.*, 1578.

Faste, eagerly, 408; close(ly), **f. by,** very near to, very close, 618.

Fain, glad, 1579; gladly, 399.

Feeld, field, 28; 119, see note.

Fe(e)re, fear, 475.

Fe(e)ste, feast, 1339; festivities, 25; festal day, 48.

Fel, see **Falle(n).**

Felawe, member of a party *or* company, 32; companion, 173; **the**

other (of the pair), 1766.

Felaweshipe, have f., keep company, 768.

Feld, *p.p.,* felled, 2066.

Fel(le), cruel, terrible, 701.

Felonye, villainy, treachery, 1138.

Fer, far, 790.

Ferde(n), see **Fare(n).**

Ferforthly, completely, 102.

Fermacies, medicines, 1855.

Fer(re), Ferrer, further, 1202; **f. ne ner,** no later or sooner, 992.

Fet, *p.p.,* fetched, 1669.

Fey, faith, **by my f.** = 'believe me,' 268.

Fiers(e), fierce, proud, brave, 740.

Fighteth, imp., 1701.

Figure, image, 1058, diagram, 1177(see note); arrangement, 1185.

Fil(len), see **Falle(n).**

Finde, *v.,* find, provide, 1555; **finden,** *pr. pl.,* 769; **fo(o)nd,** *pt. s.,* 1532; **(y)founde(n),** *p.p.,* 353.

Firy, fiery, 635.

Fleete, 1 *pr. s.,* float, 'swim,' 1539.

Fletinge, floating, 1098.

Flikeringe, *prp.,* fluttering, 1104.

Flotery, disordered, 2025.

Flour, flower, 2070; **f. of chivalrye,** the choicest knights, 124.

Foineth, *pr. s.,* thrusts with a weapon, 1757; **foine,** *pr. s. subj.,* let him thrust, 1692; **foinen,** *pr. pl.,* 796.

Folk, people, 47; **the f.,** (Creon's) people, army, 130.

Folwen, *pr. pl.,* follow, 1824; *pt. pl.,* 1293.

Folye, dooth f., acts foolishly, 2187.

Fomy, flecked with foam, 1648.

Foo, foe, 732.

Fo(o)nd, see **Finde.**

Footmen, men on foot, 1870.

For, *conj.,* because, for, since, 64; in order that, 2021; **f. as much,** inasmuch as, 750.

For, *prep.,* for, 21; out of, 83; in spite of, 1887; *with* to + *inf.,* in order to, to, 127; **for which,** wherefore, 302; **for al,** in spite of, 1162; **what for . . . and for . .,** partly by . . . partly by, 595; **for me,** as far as I am concerned, 2066.

Forbere, *v.,* leave alone, keep off, 27.

For-blak, intensely black, 1286, see note.

Fordo, *p.p.*, destroyed, undone, 702.

Forward, agreement, promise, 351.

Forgeten, *p.p.*, forgotten, 2196.

Formes, natures, 1455.

For-old, very old, 1284, see note.

Forpined, *p.p.*, grievously tormented, wasted away, 595.

Forthermoor, further on, 1211.

Forthre(n), *v.*, help, further, 279.

Forthy, therefore, 983.

Fortunen, *v.*, to give fortune, make fortunate or unfortunate; 2 *pr. s.*, 1519.

Foryete, 1 *pr. s.*, forgot, 1024; **foryet,** *imp.*, 1939; **foryeten,** *p.p.*, 1056.

Foryeve, 1 *pr. s.*, forgive, 960.

Fother, (cart-) load, 1050.

Foule, filthy, wicked, 2203.

Founde(n), see **Finde.**

Foundred, *pt. s.*, stumbled, fell down, 1829.

Fowel, bird, 1579.

Frakenes, freckles, 1311.

Free, free, unrestricted, unrestrained, 434.

Freend, friend, 610.

Fressh, fresh, bright, pure, 210; freshly, newly, 1974; in bright, pure colours, 190.

Freten, *v.*, eat, devour, 1161; **freeten,** *p.p.*, 1210.

Fro, from, 414.

Frothen, *pr. pl.*, foam at the mouth, 801.

Fruit, outcome, benefit, 424.

Ful, fully, very, quite, 121.

Fulfille, *v*, satisfy, 460; **fulfild,** *p.p.*, filled full, 82.

Furie, tormenting spirit from hell, 1826.

Gadereth, *pr. s.*, gathers, 195; **gadered,** *p.p.*, 1325.

Gaf, see **Yeve(n).**

Gailer, gaoler, 206.

Gaineth, *pr. s.* (*with dat. of person*), avails, is of advantage, 318.

Game, fun, entertainment, match, jest, 948.

Gan, *pt. s.*, began, *or as auxiliary verb*=did, 254; **gonne,** *pt. pl., as auxiliary verb*=did, 800.

Gaude, verdant, 1221.

Ge(e)re, dress, accoutrements, equipment, tackle, 158; see note, l. 514; changeful moods, 'goings on,' 673.

Geery, changeable, moved by passing passions, 678.

Gentil, noble, *and hence* tender and kind; noble-, and kind-hearted, 94.

Gentillesse, noble, *and hence* tender and kind character, tender courtesy, 62.

Gereful, full of passing passions, changeable, 680.

Gerland, garland, 196.

Gesse, *v.*, estimate, conjecture, suppose, 1735.

Gete(n), *v.*, obtain, procure (for), 654; 'save,' 1897.

Gye, *v.*, guide, rule, 1092; *pr. s. subj.*, 1928.

Gigginge, *prp.*, fitting (shields) with straps, 1646.

Gile, deceit, guile, 1738.

Gilt, offence, guiltiness, 907.

Giltlees, innocent, 454.

Gipoun, a tight-fitting vest worn over the mail and breast plate, 1262.

Gise, manner, way, course of life, 135; **at his owene g.,** having all his own way, 931; fashion, style (of dress), 1267.

Gladere, one who gladdens, *or* cheers, 1365.

Gleede, burning coal, 1139.

Gold-hewen, *p.p.*, made of gold, 1642.

Gonne, see **Gan.**

Gooldes, marigolds, 1071.

Go(on), *v.*, go, walk, 110, 349; (1) (2) *pr. pl.*, 409; **go(o)th,** *pr. s.*, 213; *pr. pl.*, 1750; *imp.*, 1700; **go(on),** *p.p.*, 555, 663, see note.

Gost, spirit, 1910.

Governance, order, method, 455.

Governe, *pr. pl.*, rule, control, 445.

Governour, ruler, 3.

Grace, mercy, favour, 262; (favour of fortune or Providence), luck fate, 734; a favour, 1016.

Graunt, promise, 448.

Graunte, 1 *pr. s.*, consent, agree to, grant, 762.

Graunting, grant, 1581.

Gree, excellence, superiority, 1875.

Gre(e)t(e), great, large, 12; fully grown, 817; thick, stout, 218; 411, see **opinioun.**

Grene, green (colour, thing, *etc.*), 178, 652.

Gretter, greater, 5.

Greves, thickets, 637; twigs, 649.

Greveth, *pr. s.*, grieves, vexes, harms, 59.

Grevous, severe, very painful, 152.

Griffon, griffin, fabulous animal with head and wings of an eagle, 1275.

Groining, murmuring, discontent, 1602.

Gruccheth, *pr. s.*, murmurs (against), complains (of), grumbles (at), 2187; **grucchen,** 1 *pr. pl.*, 2200; **g. of,** 2204–5.

Gruf, face downward, on their faces, 91.

Habergeoun, a coat of mail ending at the hips, 1261.

Habit, bearing, behaviour (*or possibly* apparel, see note) l. 520.

Hadde, see **Have.**

Haf, *pt. s.*, heaved, lifted, 1570.

Han, see **Have.**

Hange, Honge, *v.*, hang, 1552.

Hardy, courageous, daring, 24.

Haried, *p.p.*, dragged forcibly, 1868.

Harmes, misfortunes, sufferings, 1371.

Harnais, Harneis, Herneis, armour, the entire defensive equipment of horse and rider, 148; mounting, fittings, 2038.

Hauberkes, coats of mail (cf. **Habergeoun**), 1642.

Haukes, hawks, 1346.

Have, *v.*, have, preserve, *an as auxil.*, 18; **han,** (1) *pt.pl.*, 71.

He(e)d(e), head, 196; with *pl. refce.*, 849; **Maugree his h.,** see note l. 311; **(up) on his h.,** see note, l. 486.

He(e)ld(en), see **Holde(n).**

Heele, health, well-being, 413.

Heepe, heap, 86.

Heer, hair, 191; **he(e)res, heris,** *pl.*, 530.

Heer(e), here, 986.

Heer-biforn, before now, 726.

He(e)re(n), *v.*, hear, 17; **herde,** *pt. s.*, 44; **herd,** *p.p.*, 719.

Heete, *pr. s. subj.*, promise, 1540.

Heigh(e), Hye, high, lofty, 39; supreme, 940; serious, deep, 1513; serious, great (in amount), 2055; **wonder h.,** to a great height, 2045.

Heled, *p.p.*, healed, 1848.

Helmes, helmets, 1642.

Helpe(n), *v.*, help, 292; **helpe,** *pr. s. subj.*, 269; 2 *pr. pl. subj.*, 1379; **heelp,** *pt. s.*, 793; **ther h. noght,** there's no help for it, 2175.

Hem, them, 54.

Henne, hence, 1498.

Hente, *v.*, seize, catch hold of, take, 1780; *pt. s.*, 99; **henten,** *pt. pl.*, 46; **hent,** *p.p.*, 723.

Heraud, herald, 1675; *pl.*, 159.

Herd, having hair, 1660.

Herd(e), see **He(e)re(n).**

Here, her, 563.

Heer-agains, against this, 2181.

Heris, Heeres, see **Heer.**

Herkne(n), *v.,* listen (to), 668; **herkneth,** *imp.,* 985.

Herneis, see **Harneis.**

Hert, hart, 817.

Herte, heart, 93.

Herte-spoon, pit of the stomach, 1748.

Heste, command, bidding, 1674.

Hevene, heaven, heavens, 232.

Hevenisshly, divinely, 197.

Hevinesse, grief, 1490.

Hewe, complexion, colour, 180.

Hider, hither, 939.

Hidouse, hideous, 1120.

Highte, 1 *pr. s.,* am called, 700; *pt. s.,* 2; *pt. pl.,* 2062; **hight,** *p.p.,* promised, 1614; **to h.,** to be called, 699.

Highte, height, **on. h.,** aloud, 926; **in the air,** 1749; **maked up on h.,** built up, 2061.

Him, to him, 96; himself, 551.

Himselven, himself, 619.

Hir, their, 158.

Hir(e), her, 194.

His, its, 178.

Holde(n), *v.,* hold, consider, esteem, follow, keep (an agreement *or* one's room), 1091; **he(e)ld,** *pt. s.,* 1667; **helden,** *pt. pl.,* 1659; **hoold, holdeth,** *imp.,* 1010, 1810; **(y)holde(n),** *p.p.,* 449; **h.(unto),** bound, under obligation (to), 449; **h. his wey,** go straight (to-wards), 648.

Holm, holm-oak, 2063.

Holwe, hollow, hungry, 505.

Hond, hand, 529.

Honestly, properly, 586.

Honge, see **Hange.**

Honour, (virtuous) renown, honour, dignity, 50.

Hool, whole, 2148.

Hoold, see **Holde(n).**

Hoolly, wholly, 960.

Hooly, holy, 1355.

Hoom, home, 11.

Hoost, army, 16.

Hoot(e), hot, ardent, 953; heated, 951; hotly, fervently, ardently, 879.

Hoppesteres, dancers, *used as adj.*, dancing, see note, l. 1159.

Hors, horse, 775.

Hostelries, inns, 1635.

Hou, howsoever, 536;

Humblesse, humility, 923.

Humour, see note, 517; one of the four bodily moistures which, blended together, produced a man's 'complexioun' (q.v.); **h. malencolic,** black bile.

Hunte, huntsman, hunter, 820.

Hust, *p.p.,* hushed, 2123.

Hye, see **Heigh(e).**

Hye, in h., in haste, 2121.

Hye, *v.,* hasten, 1416.

Ilke, same, 2175.

Imaginacioun, (fantastic, false) conception, 236.

Imagining, conception, 1137.

In, lodging, 1578.

In, in, 4; into, 11; **i. oon,** without ceasing, 913.

Inde, applied to all of Asia beyond Persia, 1298.

Inequal, unequal (see note, l. 1351 ff.).

Infortune, see note, l. 1163.

Iniquitee, wickedness, injustice, 82.

Inne, in, 760.

Inned, *p.p.,* lodged, 1334.

Ire, anger, 82.

Iren, iron, 218.

Jalous, jealous, 471.

Jalousye, jealousy, 441.

Japed, *p.p.,* tricked, deceived, 871.

Joinant, adjoining, see **Evene.**

Jolitee, fun, festivity; (ironic), 949.

Journee, day's journey, 1880.

Joye, happiness, 170.

Juge, judge, 854.

Justes, jousting–match, series of combats in which two knights fought with lances, 1862.

Juste, *v.,* joust, 1746; **justen,** *pr. pl.,* 1628.

Juwise, judgement, sentence, 881.

Keepe, taken k., be on his guard (?), know where he is (?), 1830; **took k.,** noticed, 531.

Kempe, coarse (hair), *e.g.,* of a whisker or eyebrow, 1276.

Kepe, 1 *pr. s.,* keep, care, take care, guard, 1380; 2 *pr. s. imp.,* 1471.

Kepere, guardian, 1470.

Kinde, nature, 1593, **al in another k.,** not at all like him, quite changed, 543.

Kinrede, relations, kindred, 428.

Kist, *p.p.,* kissed, 901.

Knarry, knotty, gnarled, 1119.

Knaves, mere servingmen, 1870.

Knighthede, knighthood, rank of a knight, 1931.

Knowe, *v.,* recognize, know, understand, 512; **knowen,** 2 *pr. pl.,* 1253; **knowe,** *p.p.,* known, been intimate *or* acquainted with, 345.

Laas, snare, 959.

Lacerte, muscle, 1895.

Ladde, *pt. s.,* led, 588; **lad,** *p.p.,* 1762.

Laft(e), see **Lefte.**

Lakked, *pt. s. impers.,* lacked, 1422.

Large, wide, broad, large, 28; **at thy (his) l.,** at liberty, free, 425, see note, l. 1430.

Largely, fully, 1050.

Las, see **Laas.**

Lasse and moore, (lesser and greater), all, 898.

Lat, see **Lete.**

Launde, glade, lawn, field, 833.

Laurer, laurel, 169.

Lay, see **Lith.**

Layneres, straps, laces, **with l. lacinge,** with the fastening up of straps, 1646.

Lechecraft, art of healing, medicine, 1887.

Le(e)ne, lean, thin, 504.

Leepe, *pt. s.,* leapt, 1829.

Leeste, least, 843; **atte l. weye,** at least, 263; **meeste and l.,** see **Meeste.**

Leet, see **Lete.**

Leeve, dear, 278.

Leeveth, *imp.,* believe, 2230.

Lefte, Lafte, (1) *pt. s.*, remained, left, forsook, left off, ceased, omitted, 34; **(y)laft,** *p.p.*, 1158.

Leid(e), *pt. s. refl.* and *p.p.*, laid, 526.

Leiser, leisure, 330.

Lene, *imp.*, give, 2224.

Lenger, longer, 718.

Leopard, leopard, 1328.

Leoun, lion, 740.

Lese, *v.*, lose, 357.

Lesinges, falsehoods, deceits, 1069.

Lest, List, pleasure, delight, 2126.

Leste, see **List.**

Lete, *v.*, let, leave, forsake, 477; 1 *pr. s.*, 15; **leet,** *pt. s.*, 348; **lat, let,** *imp.*, 32; **l. se,** let us see, 33; **l. crye,** caused to be proclaimed, 1873; **l. comande,** caused orders to be given, 2007.

Letten, *v.*, hinder, delay, 31; **lette,** *pt. s.*, 1034; **l. of,** give up, forego, 459.

Leve, leave, permission, 206.

Leye, *v.*, lay, 2008.

Liche-wake, watch over a corpse, 2100.

Lief, dear, 979.

Lifly, in a life-like way, 1229.

Liggen, *pr. pl.*, lie, 1347; **ligginge,** *prp.*, 153.

Light(e), bright, shining, 925.

Lightly, cheerfully, 1012.

Ligne, line, 693.

Lik, like, 443.

Liketh, *pr. s. impers.*, **yow l.,** it pleases you, you like, 989; **him liked,** *pt. s.*, 1234.

Limes, limbs, 1277.

Linage, (ancestry), family, 252.

Linde, lime-tree, 2064.

List, see **Lest.**

List, *pr. s. impers.*, **him (me, thee, yow) l.,** it pleases him (me, etc.) 269; **leste, liste,** *pt. s.*, 146; **liste,** *pt. s. subj.*, 349.

Listes, palisades enclosing tilting-ground, tilting-ground, 855.

Lite, little, 335.

Litel, little, 426.

Lith, *pr. s.*, lies, lodges, camps, is, 937; 360, see **Wedde; lay,** *pt. s.*, 79.

Live, on l., alive, 2181.

Lives, *adv.*, in life, *thus as adj.*, living, alive, 1537.

Long, tall, 566.
Longen, *v.*, belong, be appropriate to, 1420
Loode-sterre, loadstar, the pole-star, 1201.
Lo(o)ken, *v.*, look, 925; **lo(o)keth,** *imp.*, 940.
Looking, glance, 1313.
Looth, loath, hateful, 979.
Los, loss, 1685.
Losten, 1 *pt. pl.*, lost, 78.
Lough, Lowe, low, 253; infernal, 1441.
Love, a beloved one, 1448.
Lust, joy, pleasure, desire, 392.
Lustily, joyfully, vigorously, 671.
Lusty, joyful, lively, vigorous, gay, 655.
Lustinesse, joy, gaiety, vigour, 1081.

Maad, see Make(n).
Maat, downcast, sorrowful, 97. (Persian *shāh māt*, 'the king is helpless' (*mate* in *check-mate*).)
Made, see Make(n).
Maintene, *v.*, maintain, 583; uphold, stand by, 920.
Maister strete, main street, 2044.
Maist(ow), see May.
Make, mate, 'opposite number,' 1698.
Make(n), *v.*, make, compose, draw up, cause, 196; **(y)maked, maad,** *p.p.*, 613; **m. a vanisshinge,** vanished, 1502.
Manace, threat, menace, 1145.
Manasinge, threatening, 1177.
Maner(e), kind (of), 1017; manner, 1362; **the m. how,** the way in which, how, 18–19; **in m. of,** in the fashion of, like, 1031.
Manhede, courage, valour, 427.
Manly, boldly, courageously, 129.
Manie, mania, 516.
Mantelet, short mantle, 1305.
Mapul, maple-tree, 2065.
Mat(e)ere, matter, affair, 559; state of things, 401.
Matrimoigne, matrimony, 2237.
Maugree, see note, l. 311; in spite of, 749, 938, 1760.
May, *pr. s.*, is able to, has power to, may (well), 174; **mayst,** 2 *pr. s.,* 385; **maystow** (=**mayest thou**), 378; **mowe,** *pr. pl.*, 2141.
Meeste and leeste (greatest and least), all, 1340.
Meete, meet, befitting, 1433.

Meeth, mead, 1421.

Meinee, household, retinue, 400.

Memorye, memory, remembrance, 1048; **in m.,** conscious, 1840.

Men, *indef. pron.* (*cf.* Fr. *on*), one (unstressed form of **Man**), 1022, 1337.

Mencioun, mention, 35.

Mene, 1 *pr. s.*, mean, intend, 815.

Merye, Mirye, Mury(e), merry, happy, gay, pleasant, 528.

Meschaunce, misfortune, bad luck, 1151.

Mescheef, Meschief, harm, 468; **at m.,** at a disadvantage, 1693.

Messager, messenger, 633.

Mester, Mystier, occupation, 482; **what m. men,** what kind of men (men of what calling), 852.

Mete, meet, fit, 773.

Mete, food, meat, 503.

Ministre, servant, **m. general,** chief executor, 805.

Minour, miner, 1607.

Mirre, myrrh, 2080.

Mirye, see **Merye.**

Misboden, *p.p.*, ill-used, injured, 51.

Misfille, *pt. s. subj. impers.*, it went amiss (with you), 1530.

Mishappe, *pr. s. subj. impers.*, **if that me m.,** if it go badly for me, 788.

Mo, more (in number), 171.

Moerdre, murder, 398.

Mone, moan, 508.

Moone, moon, 1219.

Montaunce, value, 712.

Mood, anger, 902.

Moore, more, 90; greater, 1966; **withouten (any) m.,** without more ado *or* delay, 683; **lasse and m.,** see **Lasse.**

Moorninge, mourning, 2110.

Mooste, greatest, 37.

Moot, 1 *pr. s.*, must, may, am permitted, 27; **moot(e),** *pr. s.*, must, ought, is bound to, 311.

Morwe, morning, 634; **in a m. of May,** one May morning.

Morweninge, morning, 204.

Mosel, muzzle, 1293.

Mowe, see **May.**

Muchel, much, 12.

Mury(e), see **Merye.**

Mystier, see **Mester.**

Nail, nail, 1149; claw, 1283.

Nakers, kettle-drums, 1653.

Nam (=ne am), 1 *pr s.*, 1953; **n. but deed,** am no better than a dead man, 264.

Name, name, 698; reputation, fame, 579

Namely, especially, 410.

Namo, no more (in number), 731.

Namoore, no more, 116.

Nas (=ne was), was not, 358.

Nat, not, 31.

Natheless, nevertheless, 974.

Naught, not at all, nothing, 1210.

Ne, not (often only intensifying negative), 65; nor, 111.

Nedes, necessarily, of necessity, 311; **n. cost,** of necessity, 619.

Nedeth, *impers. pr. s.*, (it) is necessary, 888; **what n.,** what is the need of, 171.

Ne(e)r, near, nearer, 110.

Nercotikes, narcotics, 614.

Nere (=ne were), *pt. s. subj.*, were not, would not be, 17.

Nexte, nearest, *i.e.*, quickest, 555; next, 1509.

Nis (=ne is), is not, 43.

Noght, not, 698; **n. but,** only, 1372–1373.

Nolde (=ne wolde), would not, 45; refused (to take), 166.

Nombre, number, 1738.

Nones, Nonis, for the n., specially, particularly, 21; (a mere tag— 'believe me'), 565.

Noon, none, 31; no, 68; nil, 320.

Noot (=ne woot), (1) *pr. s.*, know not, 181.

Norisshinge, growing up, 2159.

Nothing, no whit, in no way, 661.

Ny, near(ly), close(ly), 472.

O, one, a, 354, 1033.

Obsequies, funeral rites, 135.

Observaunce, keeping of a law or duty, 458; (customary) rite, 187, 1406; dutiful service, 187.

Of, of, 3; from, 45; in, 2015; as to, concerning, 25; by, 105; some (of), 2225; with, on account of, 636; off, 1818.

Offence, injury, 225.

Offende, *pr. pl.*, harm, 2207; *p.p.*, injured, attacked, 51.

Offensioun, hurt, 1558. (=It. *offensione*, *Tes.* VII. 28.)

Office, fil in o., got by chance a position, 560; rite, 2054; **o. funeral** (*=offiium funal*), 2005.

Ofte(n), often, **o. sithe(s),** often, 1019.

Olde, known from of old, 1610.

Ones, once, 176.

Ook, oak, 844.

Oon, one; **that o.** the one, 155; the same, 154; **in o.,** see **In**; **o. and oother,** in pairs, 1715.

Oonly, alone, 731.

O(o)ther(e), the other, 41; **ther is noon o.,** there is nothing else for it, 324.

Opie, opium, opiate, 614.

Opinioun, opinion, belief, conclusion, 235; **greet o.,** confident belief, 411.

Ordeined, *p.p.*, fixed, provided, 1695.

Ordinaunce, provision, decree, control, 2154; **by o.,** in battle array, in proper order, 1709.

Ordre, ordering, 2145; **by o.,** in order, 1076.

Orison, prayer, 1403.

Oth, oath, 101.

Outhees, outcry, alarm, 1154.

Outher, either, 627.

Outran, *p. pl.,* ran out, 1481.

Outrely, utterly, absolutely, outright, plainly, 296.

Over, beyond, 705; over, 835.

Overal, everywhere, 349.

Overcaste, *v.,* upset, make gloomy, 678.

Overthwart, across, 1133.

Owene, own, 794.

Pa(a)s, pace, 2043; yards, 1032; **a p.,** at walking pace, 1359.

Pace, *v.,* go on living, 2140.

Paleis, palace, 1341.

Pan, skull, 307.

Paramour(s), passionately, devotedly, constantly; **to love p.,** to love as a lover, 297.

Pardee (*=par dieu*), certainly, 'upon my word,' (a common oath), 454.

Parement(s), rich garments, like dalmatics, worn over armour, 1643.

Parfit, Perfit, perfect, 413.

Parlement, deliberation, decree, 448; deliberative assembly, 2112.

Part, share, 320; **parte,** side, party, 1724; **have . . . p.,** take the side of, protect, 1934.

Party, variegated, 195.

Partye, participator, prejudiced umpire, 1799; portion, part, 2150.

Passant, surpassing, **p. name,** name above all others, pre-eminent fame, 1249.

Passe(n), *v.,* pass, go on, 3 *pr. s.,* 175; surpass, 2231.

Paien, pagan, 1512.

Pees, peace, 589.

Peine, torture, 275; pain, grief, 439; **upon p. of,** on pain of, 849.

Peinten, *v.,* paint, 1229.

Penaunce, punishment, pain, suffering, 457.

Penoun, small, pointed flag, 120, see note.

Perfit, see **Parfit.**

Perles, pearls, 1303.

Perrye, precious stones, jewellery, 2078.

Perturben, 2 *pr. pl.,* disturb, throw into confusion, 48.

Pestilence, plague, 1611.

Physic, medical treatment, 1902.

Pighte, *pt. s. refl.,* pitched, fell, 1831.

Pikepurs, pickpocket, 1140.

Piler, pillar, 1135.

Pilours, plunderers, 149.

Pine, torment, suffering, 466.

Pine, *v.,* torture, 888.

Pipen, *v.,* pipe, 980.

Pitee, pity, 62.

Pitous, full of pity, tender, 95; pitiful, arousing pity, 97.

Pitously, pitifully, 91; piously, devoutly, 1405.

Place, field (of tourney), 1541.

Plain=Plein.

Plat, plain, downright, 'flat,' 987.

Plein, full, plain, clear, open, 629, 1603; regular, 130, see note; fully, entirely, clearly, plainly, 606; **the short and p.,** the long and the short of it, 233.

Pleine, *v.,* complain, 462; **pleinen on,** complain of, *pr. pl.,* 393.

Pleinly, fully, openly, plainly, without embellishment, 351.

Plesaunce, pleasure, will, 713; condition of being pleased, **to been in swich p.,** to feel such joy, 1627.

Pleye(n), *v.,* play, 2101; be playful, make fun, amuse (self), 337, 269, see **Yvele.**

Pleyinge, amusement, **hadde hir p.,** was amusing herself, 203.

Point, point, 1688; part, 1908; precise matter in discussion, aim, conclusion, end, 643.

Polax, pole-axe, 1686.

Pomel, rounded top of head, 1831.

Portreitour, painter, 1041.

Portreiture, figure, diagram (?), 1178; *pl.*, paintings, drawings, 1057.

Portreyinge, picture, 1080.

Pose, 1 *pr. s.*, (will) suppose, put the case, 304.

Possibilitee, as by wey of p., considering what is possible, in the nature of things, 433.

Poure, poor, 551.

Pourely, humbly, in mean guise *or* fashion, 554.

Praye, prey, 1774.

Pre(e)sseth, *pr. s.*, presses forward, throngs, 1672.

Prescience, foreknowledge, 455.

Preeved, *p.p.*, proved, shown to be (true), 2143.

Pride, magnificence, pomp, 37.

Priketh, *pr. s.*, wounds sharply, urges, stimulates, spurs, rides, darts, 185; (*prp.*) 1650.

Pricke, point, stab, 1748.

Prime, 9 a.m., *or* early morning, 1331.

Pris, reputation, renoun, worth, prize, 1383.

Privee, secret, 1602.

Prively, secretly, 364.

Privetee, secret, private affairs, 553.

Processe, process of time, course of events, 2109.

Profreth, *pr. s.*, proffers, 557.

Progressioun, the action of proceeding from a source, 1746.

Propre, own, 2179.

Proprely, correctly, properly, 601; exactly, completely, 1929.

Proude, valiant, 1740.

Proudly, haughtily, with a superior air, 294.

Pure, very, 421.

Purveiaunce, (divine) foreknowing and direction, providence, 394.

Putten, *v.*, put, 577; **putte,** *pt. s.*, **p. in,** inserted, thrust in, 2084.

Qualm, plague, 1156.

Queint(e), *pt. s.*, and *p.p.*, quenched, put a stop to, (was) extinguished, 1463, 1476.

Queint(e), strange, odd, 673.

Questioun, discussion, 1656.

Quik(e), alive, 157.

Quiked, *pt. s.,* revived, burst into flame, 1477.

Quite, *v.,* ransom, 174.

Quitly, completely (*or* at liberty), 934.

Quod, *pt. s.,* said, 49.

Quook, *pt. s.,* trembled, shook, 718.

Rad, *p.p.,* read, 1737.

Rage, fierce blast, 1127.

Ran, *see* **Renneth.**

Ransake, *v.,* make a search, 147.

Rasour, razor, 1559.

Rather, more likely, 295; rather, 516.

Raughte, *pt. s.,* reached, 2057.

Raunsoun, ransom, 166.

Recche, *v.,* care; **I r. nat to,** I don't mind whether I ..., 540, 1387; *pr. s.,* 1539.

Recke, *I pr. s.,* care, 1399.

Reconforte, *v. refl.,* take courage *or* heart again, 1994.

Recorde, *v.,* declare as one's verdict, confirm, 887.

Redily, in a state of readiness, 1418.

Redoutinge, reverence, 1192.

Re(e)d(e), red, 117.

Reed, help, remedy, 358.

Refuge, shelter, succour, 862.

Registre, book in which regular entries are made; record of such entries, list, see note, l. 1954.

Regne, realm, dominion, 8; dominion, rule, sovereignty, 766.

Rehersing, withouten r., without repeating (the terms of the agreement), 792.

Reineth, *pr. s.,* rains, 677.

Reines, reins, 46.

Rek(e)ne, *v.,* enumerate, relate, 1075.

Remedye, way out, help (for it), 358.

Remembringe (on), *prp.,* having in mind, recalling, 643.

Remena(u)nt, rest, 30.

Renges, ranks, 1736.

Renneth, *pr. s.,* runs, finds way, runs together, 903; **renne,** *pr. pl.,* 2010; **ran,** *pt. s.,* 1121; **ronnen,** *pt. pl.,* 2067; **yronne(n),** *p.p.,* 1307; **it r. him in his minde,** it came suddenly into his mind, occurred to him, 544.

Rente, income, 585.

Rente, *pt. s.*, tore, 132.

Rentinge, tearing, 1976.

Replicacioun, reply, **withouten any r.,** without reply being allowed, 988.

Rescus, rescue, 1785.

Rese, *v.*, shake, 1128.

Reso(u)n, reason; **in his r.,** when he thought about it, 908.

Resouned of, *pt. s.*, resounded with, 420.

Respit, delay, **withouten moore r.,** straightway, 90.

Retourninge, return, 1237.

Reuled, *p.p.*, ruled, 814.

Reverence, reverence, respect, 1673.

Rewe, on a r., in a row, 2008.

Rewe, *v.*, have pity, 1524; *imp.*, 1357; *pr. s. subj.*, may (God) have pity, 1005.

Rewefulleste, most sorrowful, most full of pity, 2028.

Richesse, wealth, 397.

Ride, *v.*, ride, 15; **rit,** *pr. s.*, 116; **ride,** *pr. pl.*, 2011; **riden,** *pt. pl.*, 2039; *p.p.*, 645; **rood,** *pt. s.*, 108; **go ne r., r. or go,** see note, l. 110.

Right(e), *adj.*, straight, direct, 405.

Right, *adv.*, just, exactly, very, altogether, directly, 107. 1177.

Rightes, at alle r., at all points, in every respect, 994.

Rightful, righteous, just, 861.

Rime, *v.*, recount in verse, 601.

Ringe, *v.*, (make) ring, 1573.

Rit, see **Ride.**

Romen, *v.*, walk, wander, 241.

Ronnen, see **Renneth.**

Rood, see **Ride.**

Roos, *pt. s.*, rose, 1356.

Roreth (of), *pr. s.*, resounds (with), 2023.

Rouketh, *pr. s.*, cowers, crouches, 450.

Route, company, 31.

Routhe, (a) pity, (a) sad thing, 56; pity, 1534.

Royally, in regal splendour, 829.

Rugged, rough, shaggy, 2025.

Ruine, falling down, 1605.

Rumbel, rumbling noise, 1121.

Sad, composed, 2127; **sadly,** firmly, 1744.

Sadel-bowe, raised support at front (and back) of saddle, 1833.

Saide, see **Seye.**

Salueth, *pr. s.,* salutes, greets, 634.

Saluing, greeting, salutation, 791.

Same, of the s., in the same way, 2046.

Sangwin, blood-red, 1310.

Sarge, serge, very durable woollen cloth, 1710.

Saugh, see **Se(en).**

Saw, see **Se(en).**

Sawe, saying, 305; what is said, 668.

Sawe, Sawgh, see **Se(en).**

Sayn, see **Seye.**

Scapen, *v.,* escape, 249.

Scithia, the territory north of the Black Sea, 9.

Scriptures, (learned) writings, 1186.

Se(en), *v.,* see, look, 33; **se(e),** 1 *pr. s.,* 240; *imp.,* 943; **see(n),** *pr. pl.,* 1746; **saugh, saw, sawgh, seigh,** (1) *pt. s.,* 97; **sawe,** *pt. pl.,* 897: *seyn, p.p.,* 807 (**Seyn biforn,** had prescience of).

Se(e)n(e), visible, apparent, 66.

Seet, see **Sitte(n).**

Seetes, seats, 1722.

Seid(en), see **Seye.**

Seigh, *see* **Se(en).**

Seith, see **Seye.**

Seke(n), *v.,* seek, 1729; 1 *pr. pl.,* 408; **to s.,** if you were to seek, 1729.

Selde, seldom, 681.

Selve, self-same, 1726.

Semed, *pt. s.,* seemed, appeared, 844; **s. me,** it seemed to me, 2112.

Semely, Semily, becoming, fitting, suitable, 1102.

Semily, see **Semely.**

Sende(n), *v.,* send, grant, 2118; *imp.,* 1459; *pr. s. subj.,* let (no man) send, 1687; **sende, sente,** *pt. s.,* 113, granted, 2242; **(y)sent,** *p.p.,* 1827.

Sene, *v.,* to behold, see, 177.

Sentence, meaning, opinion, 2144; judgement, decision, 1674.

Serie, process, argument, 2209.

Sermoning, sermonizing, 2233.

Servage, servitude, 1088.

Serve, 1 *pr. s.,* serve, 285; **serven,** *pr. pl.,* 947; **(y)served,** dealt with, *p.p.,* 105.

Seten, see Sit.

Sette, 1 *pr. s.,* place, set, put, appoint, fix, count, reckon, 712; *pt. s.,* 683; (y)**set,** *p.p.,* 777.

Seuretee, guarantee, formal pledge, 746.

Seye, Seyn, *v.,* say, 293; **seyst,** 2 *pr. s.,* 747; **seystow,** dost thou say, 267; **seith,** *pr. s.,* 187; **seyen,** 1 *pr. pl.*; **sayn, seyn,** *pr. pl.,* 340; **saide, seide,** *pt. s.,* 57; **seide(n),** *pt. pl.,* 575; **seyeth,** *imp.,* 1010; **ysaid, seid,** *p.p.,* 1009.

Seyn, see Se(en),

Shal, *v. auxil.* (1) *pr. s.,* am (is) to, must, shall (be), will, 33; **shaltou,** 2 *pr. s.,* (=shalt thou) 533; **shul(len),** *pr. pl.,* 1498; **shul,** 2 *pr. pl.,* 889; **sholde,** (1) *pt. s., and pl.,* should, would, ought to, was (were) to, 104.

Shamefast, modest, 1197.

Shape, contour, 1031; form, bodily appearance, 1058.

Shape(n), *v. refl.,* plan, arrange, contrive, 1683; *p.p.,* planned, shaped, determined, 250, 367, see note.

Sheeld, shield, 1264.

She(e)ne, bright, beautiful, splendid, 114.

Shent, *p.p.,* infected, injured, 1896.

Shepne, cattle-shed, 1142.

Shere, shears, scissors, 1559.

Shet, *p.p.,* shut, 1739.

Shines, shins, 421.

Shinen, *pr.pl.,* shine, 1185.

Shiveren, *pr. pl.,* shiver, 1747.

Shode, crown of the head, 1149.

Sholde, see Shal.

Shoon, *pt. s.,* shone, 1129.

Shortly, in a short time, briefly, soon, 127.

Shot, missile, 1686.

Shrighte, *pt. s.,* shrieked, 1959.

Shuldres, shoulders, 1106.

Shul(len), see Shal.

Sighte, Providence, 814.

Sike, *v.,* sigh, 682.

Sik(e), sick, 742.

Siker, secure, certain, 2191.

Sikerly, certainly, surely, 1243.

Sin, since, 335.

Sit, *pr. s.,* sits, is situate, dwells, 741; **sitten,** *pr. pl.,* 1346; **sat, seet,** *pt. s.,* 1151; *p.p.,* **seten,** 594.

Sith, since, 72.

Sithe, see **Ofte(n).**

Sithen, before now, since, 663; afterwards, 1759.

Slak, slow, 2043.

Slawe, see **Slee(n).**

Slee(n), *v.,* slay, 364; 2 *pr. pl.,* 709; **sleeth,** *pr. s.,* 260; **sle,** 2 *pr. s. subj.,* 760; *imp.,* 863; **slow,** 1 *pt. s.,* 1608; **slough,** *pt. s.,* 122; **slawe,** (y)**slain, sleen,** *p.p.,* 85, 1698.

Sleepe, *pt. s.,* slept, 616.

Sle(e)p(e), sleep, 186.

Sleere, slayer, 1147.

Sleighte, cunning, 1090.

Slepy, inducing sleep, 529.

Slider, slippery, 406.

Slogardye, laziness, sloth, 184.

Slough, Slow, see **Slee(n).**

Slyly, skilfully, wisely, discreetly, 586.

Smerte, painful, stinging, 1367.

Smerte, me s., *pr. s. subj. impers.,* it may hurt me, 536.

Smite, *v.,* strike, 362; **smoot,** *pt. s.,* 846.

So, in such a way, 118; **s. that,** provided that, 713.

Socour, held, aid, 60.

Sodeinly, Sodeinliche, suddenly, immediately, 260.

Softe, gently, quietly, slowly, 163.

Solempnitee, observance of proper ceremony, 1844.

Som, one, 2173.

Somdel, somewhat, 1312.

Somer, summer, 479.

Somtime, once, occasionally, 810.

Sone, son, 1105.

Songe(n), *p.p.,* sung, 671.

Sonne, sun, 204; **under the s.** (a common tag), on the earth, *hence,* anywhere, 5; 839, see note; **at the s. upriste,** at sunrise, 193.

So(o)n(e), soon, 164.

So(o)ng, *pt. s.,* sang, 197.

Soor(e), wound, sore, pain, 596.

So(o)r(e), grievous, wounded, 897; sorely, 257.

Sooth, see **Sothe.**

Sorwe, sorrow, grief, 93.

Sorwen, *pr. pl.,* sorrow, grieve, 1966; **sorweth,** *pr. s.,* 1794.

Sothe, Sooth, truth, **for s.,** 663; in truth, truly, 235.

Soun, sound, 1574.

Soutil, fine, 1172; cunning, skilful, 1191. *Cf.* **subtil.**

Soverein, supreme, very high, 1116.

Space, space of time, 1038.

Spak, see **Speke(n).**

Spare, *v.,* spare, refrain; + *inf.* = from doing something, 538.

Sparre, rafter, 132; pole, bar of wood, 218.

Sparth, battle-axe, 1662.

Speces, species, kind (*or ?* essential quality), 2155.

Special, in s., in particular, distinctively, 159.

Spe(e)de, *pr. s. subj.,* may (God) prosper (you), 1700; **him spedde,** *pt. s. refl.,* hastened, 359.

Speke(n), *v.,* speak, 95; 1 *pr. s.,* 975; **spak,** (1) *pt. s.,* 54; **(y)spoken,** *p.p.,* 2114; **to s. of,** as regards, 127.

Spere, spear, 117.

Spicerye, mixture of spices, 2077.

Spores, spurs, 846.

Sprad, *p.p.,* spread, covered, 2045.

Springe, *v.,* dawn, 1351; grow, 1315; *pr. s.,* springs, jumps, 1013; **springen,** *pr. pl.,* 1749; **sponge,** *p.p.,* sprung up, gone abroad, 579.

Square, stout, strong, 218.

Squier, follower, servant, 552.

Staat, see **Esta(a)t.**

Stablissed, *pr.p.,* established, 2137.

Stalketh, *pr. s.,* walks stealthily, 621.

Starf, see **Sterve.**

Startlinge, *prp.,* leaping, bounding, 644.

Statue, image, 117.

Steede, war-horse, 1299.

Steer, bullock, 1291.

Stente(n), *v.,* stop, 1584; **stent,** *p.p.,* 510; **s. of,** leave off, 45.

Sterres, stars, 1179.

Stert, at a s., with one bound, in an instant, 847.

Sterte, *v.,* leap, spring (up), 186; **sterte, stirte,** *pt. s. refl.,* 94, 721.

Sterve, *v.,* die, 391; *pr. s. subj.,* 286; **starf,** *pt. s.,* 75; **ystorve,** *p.p.* 1156.

Stevene, time, **at unset s.,** (at an unappointed time), by chance, unexpectedly, 666; voice, sound, 1704.

Stierne, severe, grim, fiercely brave, 1296; strongly flowing, 1752.

Stille, quietly, 145.

Stinte(n), *v.*, leave off, stop, 476; **stinteth,** *imp.*, 1816; **stinte,** *pt. s.*, 1563.

Stirte, see **Sterte.**

Stith, anvil, 1168.

Stok, stock, race, family, 693; **stockes,** *pl.*, stumps of tree *or* blocks of wood, 2076.

Stoke, *v.*, stab, thrust, 1688.

Stole, *p.p.*, stolen, 1769.

Stomblen, *pr. pl.*, stumble, 1755.

Stonde(n), *v.*, stand, be, be placed, 315; be, fall out, 464.

Stongen, *p.p.*, stung, 221.

Stoon, stone, 1030.

Stout(e), strong, 1276.

Straughte, *pt. pl.*, extended, 2058.

Straunge, foreign, 'stranger,' 1860.

Stree, straw, 2060.

Streight(e), straightway, directly, 792; direct, 832.

Streit, narrow, 1126.

Stremes, beams, rays, 637; streams, 1752.

Strepe, *v.*, strip, 148.

Stroof, *pt. s.*, strove, vied, 180.

Strook, stroke, 843.

Stubbes, stumps, 1120.

Subtil, finely plaited, 196 (L. *subtilis* = finely woven).

Successiouns, by s., in succession to one another, passing from one state to another, 2156.

Suffisaunt, sufficient, 773.

Sum (=**som**), some, 230.

Sustene, *v.*, hold up, 1135.

Suster, sister, 13; **sustren,** *pl.*, 161.

Suite, of the same s., in the same material, to match, 2015.

Sweete, genial, pleasant, agreeable, fragrant, 1396.

Swelte, *pt. s. (lit.* died), was ready to die, felt faint, fainted, 498.

Swerd, sword, 357.

Swere, *v.*, swear, 963.

Swich(e), such, 4; **s. another,** another . . . of that kind, 44.

Swoote, sweet, fresh, 2002.

Sworen, *pt. pl.*, swore, 968.

Swough, sough, rushing sound of wind, etc., 1121.

Swowned, *p.p.*, fainted, swooned, 55; **swowninge,** *prp.*, 1961.

Taak, see **Take.**

Taas, heap, 147.

Table, tablet, 447.

Take, *v.*, take, 111; **ta(a)k,** *imp.*, 226; **(y)take(n),** *p.p.*, 581; **t. at herte,** consider favourably, 1368.

Tale, tale, account, 30.

Tare, seed of a vetch (hence used for any small particle), 'jot,' 712.

Targe, light shield, 117.

Tarien, *v.*, **t. forth the day,** spend all day, 1962.

Teene, vexation, annoyance, 2248.

Telle(n), *v.*, tell, give (account), 32; *pr. pl.*, 1; **telle,** 1 *pr. s. subj.*, 1406; **telleth,** *imp.*, 52; **toold,** *p.p.*, said, 290.

Terme, period, 2170; appointed period, duration, **t. of his lyve,** for the duration of his life, 171.

Testeres, head-pieces, 1641.

Thank, expression of gratitude; **hir (his) thankes,** of their (his) own accord, willingly, with all their (his) heart, 768.

Than(ne), then, 621.

That, *conj.*, that (as a consequence), so that, 43; *often subjoined to other conjs.*, e.g., **whil,** 79; *and to advs.*, e.g., **whan,** 143; **that ... ne,** but that, 1008.

That, *rel. pron.*, who, which, that, that which, 44; to whom, 1042; **that ... his,** whose, 1852; *adj.* the: **that oon,** one (of two), 155; **that oother,** the other, 156.

Ther, there, 39; where, 34; in that business, in those circumstances, 1872. **Ther as,** whereas, 460; in the place where, 126.

Therbiforn, beforehand, 1176.

Therfore, for that, on that account, 950.

Therto, for it, to it, 1251.

Therwith(al), thereupon, 220.

Thider, thither, to it, 405.

Thicke, thick, 721; solid, stout, 198; filled (with), dense, packed, 217; **thicke-herd,** [the man] having thick hair.

Thilke (=the ilke), that same, 335.

Thing, thing, matter, affair, composition, story, 27; creation, created thing, 2155; 1435, see note; *pl.*, 2178.

Thinke(1), *v.*, think (of), intend, consider, reflect; **thinketh,** *pr. s.* 785; **think,** *imp.*, 748; **tho(u)ghte,** *pt. s.*, 126. (O.E. ðenc(e)an.) In M.E. this verb was confused with **Thinke** (2).)

Thinke, (2), *v.*, *impers.*, seem; **yow thinketh,** it seems to you, 1009; **him (us) thoughte,** it seemed to him (us), 96. (O.E. ðync(e)an. In M.E. this verb was confused with **Thinke** (1).)

Thirled, *p.p.*, pierced, 1852.

Thise, these 594; (referring to a class of people or things), 673.

Tho, those, 265.

Tho, then, 135.

Thonken, *pr. pl.*, thank, 1018.

Though, yet, 1096.

Tho(u)ghte, see **Thinke** (1) and (2).

Thral, subject, in bondage, 694.

Threste, *v.*, thrust, push, 1754.

Thridde, third, 605.

Thries, thrice, 2094.

Thurgh, through, 'out of,' 62.

Thurghfare, passage, way, 1989.

Thurgh-girt, pierced through, 152.

Thurghout, through, 238.

Til, to, 274; **t. that,** until, 632.

Time, by t., betimes, early, 1717.

Tirannye, unmerciful, harsh action *or* attitude, 83.

Tiraunt, harsh ruler, 103.

To, too, 17; as, for, 431.

Too, toe, 1868.

Tobreste, *pr. pl.*, shatter, 1753; **tobrosten,** *p.p.*, 1833.

Togidre, together, 1766.

Tohewen, *pr. pl.*, hew to pieces, 1751.

Tonne-greet, wide as a tun, *or* barrel, 1136.

Tope, top, 2057.

Toshrede, *pr. pl.*, cut to pieces, 1751.

Toun, town, 36.

Tour, tower, 172.

Touret, turret, 1051.

Tourettes, swivel rings on dog collars, by which cords can be attach 1294.

Tourneyinge, tournament, 1862.

Trace, Thrace, 780.

Trais, traces, 1281.

Trapped, *p.p.*, having trappings, 1299.

Trappures, trappings, covering of a horse, 1641.

Travaille, labour, 1548.

Travaillinge, *prp.*, in labour, 1225.

Treso(u)n, betrayal, treachery, 1143.
Tretee, negotiation, 430.
Trewe, true, honest, faithful, 101.
Trewely, truly, faithfully, 279.
Trompe, trumpet, 1316.
Tronchoun, broken shaft of spear, 1757.
Trone, throne, 1671.
Trouthe, pledged word, promise, 752; **upon my t.,** upon my pledged word, 'believe me,' 997,
Trowe, 1 *pr. s.,* think, believe, ='take my word for it,' 1023; *pt. s.,* and *p.p.,* 662, 1243.
Tweine, (twain) two, 266, 276.
Tweye, two, 270; **t. and t.,** in pairs, 40.

Unconninge, ignorant, unskilful, 1535.
Uncouth, curious, strange, 1639.
Under, at the foot of, 1123.
Understonde, *v.,* understand, 2158.
Unknowe, unknown, 548.
Unset, unappointed, see **Stevene.**
Untressed, *p.p.,* let down, undone, 1431.
Unwist, u. of him, (it being) unknown by him, 2119.
Unyolden, *p.p.,* without having yielded, 1784.
Uphaf, *pt. s.,* lifted up, 1570.
Upright, lying on back, face upward, 1150.
Upriste, uprising, 193.
Up-so-doun, in(to) disorder, 519.
Upsterte, *pt. s.,* sprang up, 222.
Upyaf, *pt. s.,* gave forth, 1569.
Upyolden, *p.p.,* yielded up, 2194.
Usage, practice, custom, habit, 1590.

Vassellage, prowess, noble exploits, 2196.
Vein(e), vain, empty, false, worthless, 236.
Veine, vein, 1889.
Venerye, hunting, 1450.
Verraily, truly, 316.
Verray, *adj.,* true, 693.
Vertu, power, 1391, 1891, see note; superior qualities, manly excellence, 578.

Vese, rush, violent current, 1127.

Vileinye, a discourtesy, a shameful wrong, 84; anything shameful, boorish, or discourteous, 1871.

Voiden, *v.*, discharge, 1893.

Vomit, emetic, 1898, see note.

Waike, weak, 29.

Waiteth, *pr. s.*, watches, 364; *prp.*, waiting, 71.

Wake-pleyes, funeral games, 2102.

Wan, see **Winne(n).**

Wan, dark, gloomy, lead-coloured, 1598.

Wanhope, despair, 391, (orig. despair of the Mercy of God, and so transferred to despair of the mercy of the loved one).

Wan(i)e, *v.*, wane, 1220; decrease in size or power, 2167.

War, cautious, prudent, 360; **was w.,** noticed, 38.

Waymentinge, lamentation, 44.

Wawes, waves, 1100.

Wedde, pledge, **lith to w.,** is the guarantee, is at stake, 360.

Wede, clothing, 148.

We(e)l(e), well, very, fully, 68; satisfactorily, 968; **w. was him,** it was well for him, 1251.

Weep, see **Wepe.**

Wele, pomp, splendid array, 37; well-being, happiness, 2243; object of delight, source of happiness, 414; **in hir w.,** at their happiest, 1815.

Welle, fountain, 1425; source, 2179.

Wende(n), *v.*, go, 533, decay, 2168; **wente(n),** *pt. s.*, and *pl.*, 141.

Wene(n), *v.*, think, suppose, fancy, 797; *pr. pl.*, 946; **wende,** 1 *pt. s.*, 411.

Wepe, *v.*, weep, 437; **wepen,** *pr. pl.*, 913; **weep,** *pt. s.*, 1487; **weep,** *imp.*, 1612.

Wepene, weapon, 733.

Werche, Wirche, *v.*, do, work, perform, act, fashion, 1901; **wroghte,** *pt. s.*, 1214; **(y)wro(u)ght,** *p.p.*, 154, 1766; (see **Wo).**

Were, *pr. pl.*, wear, 2090; **wered(e),** *pt. s.*, 530.

Were, *v.*, defend, 1692.

Were(n), *pt. pl.*, were, 98; **were,** *pt. s.*, and *pl. subj.* might (would) be, 136.

Werre, war, 589; hostile attack, assault, 429.

Werreye(n), *v.*, make war, 626; war against, 686.

Wessh, *pt. s.*, washed, 1425.

Wete, wet, 422; full of sap, 1480.

Wexeth, *pr. s.*, waxes, grows, becomes, 2166; *prp.*, 1220.

Wey(e), way, road, 39.

Weyeth, *pr. s.*, weighs, 923.

Weylaway, alas!, 80.

Whan, when, 36.

Whe(i)ther, which ever (of two), 267.

Wheither, whether, 299.

Whelpe, cub, 1769.

Wher, whether, 243.

Wher, where, 39.

Wheras, where, 255.

Which(e), which, what, who, whom, 155; **w. that,** who, 73; **w a,** what kind of a, 1817; 302, see **For.**

Whil, While, while, 79.

Whilom, once upon a time, formerly, 1.

Whippeltre, cornel *or* dogwood (tree), 2065.

Wicke, harmful, baleful, evil, 229.

Wid(e), wide, wide-open, spacious, of wide extent, far-spread, 473.

Widwe, widow, 313.

Wif, woman, wife (married woman), 74.

Wight, person, 567.

Wighte, weight, 1287.

Wilfulnesse, perversity, asserting one's own will against reason, 2199.

Wil(le), wish, 246; desire, 459; will, longing (?), 2220.

Wilnen, *v.*, desire, 1256.

Wiltow, see **Wolt(e).**

Wilugh, willow, 2064.

Winne(n), win, gain, conquer, 33; (2) *pr. s. subj.*, 759; **wan.,** *pt. s.*, 131; **(y)wonne(n),** *p.p.*, 6.

Wirche, see **Werche.**

Wis, prudent, sensible, having practical ability, skilful, learned, 562.

Wis, *adv.*, certainly (apheltic form of O.E. **gewis,**=certain), 1928.

Wisdom, sound judgement, learning, 7.

Wisly, certainly, surely, 1005 (O.E. **wislice**; *cf.* **wis,** *adv.*).

Wiste(st), see **Wo(o)t.**

Wit, 'wits,' mind, mental power, 'brains,' 598.

Witen, see **Wo(o)t.**

With, with, 11; by, through, 7.

Withouten, without, 90.

Withseye, Withseyn, deny, 282.

Witing, knowledge, 753.

Wive, see **Yeve.**

Wo, lamentation, mourning, 42; sorrow, 61; **wroghte w.,** did harm to, injured, 1214.

Wodebinde, woodbine, honeysuckle, 650.

Woful, sad, sorrowful, 205.

Wol(e), (1) *pr. s.,* and *pl.,* will, desire, intend, *and as future auxil.,* 31; **woltow, wiltow,** 2 *pr. s.* (= **wilt thow**), 298; **wolt,** 2 *pr. s.,* 737; **woln,** *pr. pl.,* 1263; **woldestow,** 2 *pt. s.* (= **woldest thow**), 1977; **wolde,** 1 *pt. s. subj.,* should like to, 1182.

Wommanhede, 'womanhood,' womanliness, 890.

Wonder, wondrous, 1215; wondrously, extremely, 796.

Wone, custom, wont, 182.

Woneden, *pt. pl.,* dwelt, lived, 2069.

Wonne(n), see **Winne(n).**

Wont, *p.p.,* accustomed, wont, 337.

Wood, mad, 471.

Woodly, madly, fiercely, 443.

Woodnesse, madness, 1153.

Wook, *pt. s.,* awoke, 535.

Wo(o)t, (1) *pr. s.,* 282, 3 *pr. s.,* 28 know(s); **woost;** 2 *pr. s.,* 316; **wootow,** do you know? 305; **wiste,** *pt. s.,* 418; **wistest,** 2 *pt.s.,* 298; **witen,** (1) *pr. pl.,* 402.

World, mankind, everybody, 808.

Worshipful, honourable, 577.

Worthy, excellent, distinguished (*esp.* for military skill *or* by position in society), 143 (it is often difficult to distinguish this sense from the following); suitable, having the appropriate or suitable qualities, 383, 1522.

Wostow, see **Wo(o)t.**

Wowke, week, 681.

Wrecche, unfortunate *or* sorrowful person, 73.

Wrecched, unfortunate, miserable, 63.

Wreke, *v.,* avenge, 103.

Wrethe, wreath, 1287.

Write, *v.,* write (of, about), 343; **writen,** *pr. pl.,* 447; *p.p.,* 1492.

Wrothe, angry, at variance, at each others' throats, 321.

Wro(u)ght(e), see **Werche.**

If a *p.p.* prefixed by **y** cannot be found in this section look for the body of the word under the appropriate letter. Thus for **ycleped** look under **clepen.**

Yaf, see **Yeve.**

Ybete, *p.p.,* see note, l. 121.

Ybore, Yborn, see **Bere.**

Ybounden, see **Binde.**

Ybroght, see **Bringe(n).**

Yburied, *p.p.,* buried, 88.

Yclenched, *p.p.,* strengthened with bars, 1133.

Ycorve, *p.p.,* cut, 1155.

Ydropped, *p.p.,* sprinkled with drops, 2026.

Yeer, Yere, year, 175; *pl.,* 2109.

Yelpe, *v.,* boast, 1380.

Yemen, *pl.,* attendants, 1651.

Yerde, stick, rod, 529; yard (length), 192.

Yere, see **Yeer.**

Yet, y. now, just now, 298; **ne y.,** and also not, 1084.

Yeve(n), Yive, *v.,* give, 306; *imp.,* 862; **yif,** *imp.,* 1402; **gaf, yaf,** *pt. s.,*
583; **yeven,** *p.p.,* 57; **y. to wive,** (give as wife), grant in marriage,
1002.

Yfetered, *p.p.,* fettered, 371.

Yfounde(n), see **Finde.**

Ygrounde, *p.p.,* ground, sharpened, 1691.

Yiftes, gifts, 1340.

Yif, Yive, see **Yeve.**

Ylaft, *p.p.,* left, 1888.

Yliche, Ylik, alike, equally, 1668.

Ylik(e), like, 681.

Ymeind, *p.p.,* mixed, 1312.

Ymet, *p.p.,* met, 1766.

Yno(u)gh, enough, plenty, 30.

Yolle, *pr. pl.,* yell, 1814.

Yond, yonder, 241.

Yore, formerly, for a long time, **ful y. agoon,** a very long while ago,
955; **of y. agon,** of long ago, 1083.

Youling, loud crying, 420.

Yow, (to) you, 51; *refl.,* yourself, 247.

Ypaied, *p.p.,* paid, 944.

Yraft, *p.p.,* robbed, snatched, torn away, 1157.

Yronne(n), see **Renneth.**

Ysaid, see **Seye.**

Yslain, see **Slee(n).**

Yspreind, *p.p.,* sprinkled, 1311.

Ystiked, *p.p.,* stuck, stabbed, 707.

Ystorve, see **Sterve.**

Ysworn, *p.p.*, sworn, 274.

Yturned, *p.p.*, directed, caused to move *or* fall reversed(?), 380; **y. til,** changed into, 1204.

Yvele, hardly, with difficulty, **me list ful y. pleye,** I'm scarcely in the mood for jesting, 269.

Ywonne(n), see **Winne(n).**

Ywroght, see **Werche.**

Ywrye, *p.p.*, covered, 2046.

ADDITIONAL NOTES

1. (See f.n. 1). *Cf.* also *A Midsummer Night's Dream*, I.i. 167 ("To do observance to a morn of May") with *K.T.* 189, 642.

28–29. The metaphor of ploughing for writing or composing is found in medieval Latin and early vernacular literature.

233. *This is:* contracted into one syllable (*cf.* 885) and hence sometimes written *this:* v. 1905n.

243. In the *Teseida* both lovers ask each other whether Emilia is goddess or earthly woman (III. 26). Cf. *Troilus and Criseyde* I, 425–426, and Skeat's note thereon.

470. Astrology specifically associated Saturn with imprisonment: *cf.* l. 1599.

676 ff. According to Alexander Neckam (1157–1217), Friday is "almost always" different from the rest of the week because Venus, as a warm and moist planet, has to provide warmth or rain to compensate for their absence on other days: it being a function of this 'benevolent' and 'benign' planet to give pleasurable change to mankind. (The conceit of ll. 1807–8 depends on the 'humid' quality of Venus.)

708. A similar expression occurs in a Durham book, *Dobsons Drie Bobbes* (1607): "as a man should say, predestined unto him before either coat or shirt."

805. *ministre general.* The phrase is evidently adapted from Dante, *Inferno* VII, 78, where Virgil states that God has ordained Fortune as "general ministra educe." *Troilus and Criseyde* V, 1541–44 (see main note) is likewise derived from *Inferno* VII, 938. See note to l. 311.

959. *As he that.* 'Being myself one who . . .'; the construction is based on the French idiom 'comme celui qui.'

1083 ff. Chaucer's lists of lovers are discussed by J. A. W. Bennett, *The Parlement of Foules* (1957), p. 101.

1097 ff. The description of the statue of Venus closely resembles those of the goddess given by medieval mythographers, in particular in Albericus's *De Deorum Imaginibus*; but Chaucer substitutes a cittern (*cythara*) for the shell that she usually carries. Music is the 'food of love', and this particular instrument was perhaps assigned to Venus because of a supposed association of its name with her island of Cythera. See also John M. Steadman in *Speculum* XXXIV (1959), p. 620.

1183 ff. The description corresponds to that given by Albericus (see 1189 n.) and to pictures of Mars in medieval MSS, which show him standing on a cart and accompanied by a wolf.

1255. *Engelond:* a weakened form of *Engla lond*, 'the land of the English': hence -*e*- constitutes a syllable. Cf. *C.T. Prol.* 16.

1423. For a similar use of 'smoking' *cf.* Chaucer's *Complaint of Mars*, 124 ('Derk was this cave, and smoking as the helle').

1598. Most of the misfortunes here listed are ascribed to Saturn by one medieval authority or another: for 'prison' *cf.* l. 470; for 'pestilence', *Piers Plowman* C, IX. 348 ff.

1675, 1741. The conduct of tournaments was the primary function of heralds.

1855. *save.* A verse introduction to a fifteenth-century medieval tract claims that wounds made by any weapon may be cured by drinking 'save or antioche' (another potion):

> Be that 21 daies be come and gon
> He shal ben hole bothe flesche and bon.

1900–1. Nature, says Albert the Great (1193–1280) acts against disease by dispersing, dividing, or expelling the cause of it. (*Opera* (1952) xii. 234).

1989–91. The lines may be regarded as an answer to Arcite's question in l. 1919. The figure of life as a pilgrimage (a medieval commonplace) is found in Latin writers (*e.g.*, Seneca) as well as in Hebrews XI, 13, I Peter II, 11, etc.

2130. *the faire cheine of love.* In the *Roman de la Rose* (16786–7). Nature as deputy of God is depicted as ceaselessly renewing the links of "la bele chaiene doree qui les quatres elemenz enlace" by perpetuating "fourmes" (cf. *species, K.T.* 2155).

For further discussion of the topic see Bennett, *The Parlement of Foules*, pp. 124–5.

2184. *To maken vertu of necessitee:* 'to submit gracefully to the inevitable.' The phrase is modelled on French 'faire de necessite vertu'; it is first found in the works of St Jerome.

2186. *that to us alle is due:* 'that which pertains to us all by necessity'—viz., death: *cf.* Acts of Henry VII, 7, c. 12 (Preamble): "Death is due to every creature born in this world."

SUGGESTIONS FOR FURTHER READING:

Hammond, E. P.: *Chaucer, A Bibliographical Manual* (1908, 1933). See especially the sections on Language and Verse pp. 481 ff.).

Brewer, D. S.: *Chaucer* (1953).

Coghill, N.: *Geoffrey Chaucer* (British Council Pamphlet, 1956).

Curry, W. C.: *Chaucer and the Mediaeval Sciences* (2nd ed. 1960). See especially pp. 130–7 on the astrological significance of the descriptions of Lycurgus and Emetreus, and pp. 139–48 on the death of Arcite.